M000105398

Under His Wings

WORKBOOK

...truths to heal adopted, orphaned,
fostered and waiting children's hearts

" ...like an eagle that stirs up its nest

and hovers over its young,

that spreads its wings to catch them

and carries them on its pinion. "

Deuteronomy 32:11

by Sherrie Eldridge & Beth Willis Miller

Published by Jewel Among Jewels Adoption Network, Inc.
www.SherrieEldridge.com
mail@sherrieeldridge.com
bethwillismiller@gmail.com

Copyright © 1999, 2000, 2004, 2012 by Jewel Among Jewels Adoption Network, Inc.
All rights reserved. No part of this manual may be published or reproduced in any manner
whatsoever without written permission from the authors.

♦

♦

Excerpt from *Destiny and Deliverance: Spiritual Insights on the Life of Moses*, by Phillip
Yancy, Max Lucado, John C. Maxwell, Jack Hayford, Joni Eareckson Tada, Tommy Barnett,
Kenneth Boa and Thelma Wells. Printed with permission of Thomas Nelson Publishers.

All Scripture quotations, unless otherwise indicated, are taken from the HOLY BIBLE, NEW
INTERNATIONAL VERSION®. NIV®. Copyright © 1973, 1978, 1984 by International
Bible Society. Used by permission of Zondervan Publishing House. All rights reserved.

Copyright © 2012 Jewel Among Jewels Adoption Network, Inc.

All rights reserved.

ISBN: 978-0-615-62921-6

DEDICATION

Dedicated to the late Pastor Russ Blowers and the late Pastor Gary Rowe.

Both were instrumental in encouraging the original writing of this workbook

for use with adoption groups at East 91st Street Christian Church, Indianapolis, Indiana.

Dedicated to YOU!

May you discover the safest place in the world to share your feelings

about adoption, orphanage, and foster care experiences—

under God's wings!

A Letter to You

Dear friend,

Ever get angry? Ever feel uncontrollable rage? Ever wonder if your level of anger is pathologic, that there's something inherently wrong with you? Ever feel like your emotions are out of proportion to the circumstances? Like us, you may weep longer and louder at stranger's funeral than the deceased person's family. Where does all this seemingly uncontrollable emotion come from?

Why do many of us see life through a lens of rejection? Why do unanswered phone calls, emails, and letters spell R-E-J-E-C-T-I-O-N to us? Will we ever get over it? Why is our self-esteem not low, but non-existent? Why do we try to be like others instead of being ourselves? Do we even know who we are? Why are we afraid we'll be too much to handle and why are goodbye's so difficult? Why do we have meltdowns on birthdays when everyone is kind? Why aren't their efforts ever enough to please us?

Why do many of us go from therapist to therapist and not find the help we need? Is there anybody out there who "gets it?" Can *anyone* hear? Who can understand what happens inside us when we lose our first family, second, third or fourth family? Who can understand what we experience when we are placed for the 29th time in a foster home, or suffer abuse in a county home or orphanage, or "age out" of the foster care system? Is there anyone who can understand?

Yes! There are *many* that fit the description and you will hear their voices as you read the pages in this workbook. You will discover that you're not alone. You will discover that being in their presence just one hour is better than years of therapy.

Finding fellow strugglers on the journey is not enough, however. It's a huge step in the right direction toward healing, but what about our deep wounds? Wounds that we may not be able to describe? Wounds that make us feel crazy and unapproachable? Wounds like hearing we were conceived in the worst possible situation. Wounds that cloud our belief system to the point that we believe our lives are a mistake. Wounds that tell us we were never worth anything, anyway. Wounds that tell us that we deserve rejection from our first family? How can we know the reason why we've had disruptions in our family?

Can we ever have peace when we've experienced such a painful past?

There's only one way to find peace with a painful past and that is through a personal relationship with God through faith in Jesus Christ. He alone, through His Spirit, can place a healing balm on our deep wounds. The Bible says: "You can't heal a wound by saying it's not there!" (Jeremiah 6:14 TLB)

We (Beth and Sherrie) have found that in the places that hurt the most, God brings a promise from the Bible to our memory at just the right time. We have experienced comfort and growth through our growing relationship with Jesus and how we long for the same growth for you!

You may be thinking, "Fine for Beth and Sherrie, but I know nothing about a personal relationship with God. I've never picked up a Bible, let alone know a verse well enough to bring it to mind."

That's okay. Wherever you are in your journey is exactly where you should be and the fact that you've picked up this workbook shows that your heart wants to be healed.

The Biblical account describing God as an eagle teaching his eaglets to fly is exactly the process you'll go through as you work through the chapters of the workbook. "Like an eagle that stirs up its nest and hovers over its young, that spreads its wings to catch them and carries them on its pinions." (Deut. 32: 11).

Now, let's apply this verse by envisioning God as the eagle and yourself as one of the eaglets in his nest.

First, he stirs up our nest by taking away the soft things in life. Losing our first family, being passed by in foster care or the orphanage, being rejected when you finally find your birth mother.

We complain to God and everyone within earshot. We don't like the pain. Why did we have to hurt like this? Why can't we have a normal childhood? Why all the chaos and change?

Then, God the eagle hovers over us, showing us the magnificence of his wings—his strength, majesty, power, and sovereignty. If little eaglets could talk, they'd say, "We never knew you were so big and powerful."

Notice that the eaglet's attention is drawn away from the painful nest to God's wings. Like eaglets, we want to know him more when we begin to discover his awesomeness is the pages of Scripture.

After we have rested beneath his wings and allowed healing to begin, God invites us to ride on His wings, away from a painful past into an incredibly wonderful future.

Are you ready to rest under his wings?

Wherever you are in your journey, we are honored that we can walk with you for a while!

With Love and Hugs,

Sherrie and Beth

What the Workbook Is About

This workbook is intended to help you determine what impact separation from your first family has had on your present day life. This won't be an ethereal exercise. It will be practical so that you will know beyond a doubt that you have worked through your painful past. Then, chapter titles will reflect the thoughts you'll have once growth has begun. How exciting is that?

Prepare to be challenged! Studying the Bible will be an integral part of each chapter because we don't wasn't you to put a bandaid on a gaping wound. Complete healing cannot occur apart from God. If you have never studied the Bible, we suggest purchasing an easy-to-understand version, such as the *New Living Translation*. Be sure to bring your Bible with you if you're using this material in a group or with a counselor or parent. Don't worry if you aren't familiar with the Bible. We will help you!

Prepare to make life-changing decisions also. You will be asked at the end of every chapter, *"What is the take-away? How is my life going to change as a result of studying and applying what I have learned in this chapter?"*

For maximum growth, be sure to complete every chapter. The old adage, "You get out of it what you put into it" is true here.

Part I reveals thoughts that indicate you may have buried emotions about separation from your first family that need to be healed. They are:

- "I feel like something's missing."
- "I often feel like I don't belong."
- "I blow up easily and hurt others."
- "I sometimes fantasize about my birth family."
- "I am confused about my identity."
- "I push myself to be perfect."
- "I am terrified of rejection."
- "I struggle with self-esteem."
- "I get uptight whenever I think about meeting my birth family."

Part II reveals thoughts that indicate you have come to terms with your adoption/foster/orphanage experience. They are:

- "I have a unique life purpose...I can see how God is working in my life!"
- "I can now take rejection in stride!"
- "I can now see my adoption experience through God's eyes!"

Now that we've seen the overview of the workbook, let's take a closer look at what we can expect in every chapter.

How Each Chapter Is Divided...

Each chapter is divided into ten sections:
*   The Scriptural Base for the Moses Narrative
*   The Story of Moses
*   How Moses Saw God
*   How You See God
*   How Other Adoptees Feel
*   Learning About Adoption
*   Putting My Feelings and Needs into Words
*   Writing a Letter TO and FROM My Birth Mother
*   Digging Deep for Answers to My Adoption Questions
*   Thoughts, Insights, Goals and Prayers

Here is a brief description of each chapter's sections:

The Scriptural Base for the Moses Story

Because Scripture is God-breathed, it is important for you to read the Scripture before you begin each chapter. Say a short prayer like this: "God, please make yourself real to me as I read." As you read, there may be words that seem like they're written in neon or phrases that pop out to you because they parallel something that is occurring in your life. This is likely God speaking to you through His Word!

The New International Version of the Bible is quoted unless otherwise indicated.

The Story of Moses

You will likely identify with Moses, an adoptee who lived in biblical times and whose life history comes alive in the pages of Scripture! He will serve as our journey mate, our encourager. Because Moses' detailed life narrative is not recorded in Scripture, we'll use a sanctified imagination to fill in the blanks.

How Moses Saw God

Each chapter will introduce a different name for God, which reveals Moses' growing relationship with Him. Don't be surprised if your spiritual appetite for reading the Bible increases and your desire for intimacy and friendship with God is deepened.

How You See God

Each chapter will refer you to the List of Jesus' Names in Scripture in Appendix B. You will then select three to five names for God that stand out to you. It will be encouraging to look back when finished with the workbook and see how your perception has grown!

How Other Adoptees Feel

This section contains quotes from fellow adoptees who have courageously revealed their honest feelings about their adoption experiences so that you can know you're not alone. In fact, you're in great company.

Learning about Adoption

Learning how adoption affects you and your family is a key to having healthy relationships with others. In this section, adoption specialists, authors and mental health professionals offer insights and practical ways of dealing with the issue presented in each chapter.

Putting My Feelings and Needs into Words

In this section you will be challenged to wrap words around your feelings. This is often difficult if emotions have been repressed. If you lost your birth mother as a baby, it will be difficult to describe your feelings because they are sensory memories. If you lost your first mother when you were older or never had a mother because you were in an orphanage, you will have no trouble remembering what occurred in our heart and home. Hearing fellow adoptees share will help you not only identify but also verbalize those feelings.

Writing a Letter TO and FROM My Birth Mother

Many adoption professionals say that writing letters TO and FROM the birth mother is the most effective way of getting in touch with buried feelings. You will be asked to do this in each chapter and periodically you will be asked to write letters to your adoptive parents/foster parents/care giver, and to God. You need not be afraid that you will have to read these letters aloud. You are in charge of when and where you want to share.

Digging Deep for Answers to My Adoption Questions

This section will ask you to dig into your Bible for answers and then challenge you to apply them to your life. Isaiah 55:2 says, "Why spend money on what is not bread, and your labor on what does not satisfy? Listen, listen to me, and eat what is good, and your soul will delight in the richest of fare."

Thoughts, Insights, Goals and Prayers

Recording your journey will lift you during times of discouragement. You will be able to look back and see how much growth has occurred.

This concludes our section-by-section explanation. Now let's talk about where and how to begin.

Instructions for Beginning

For individual work—Use the workbook at your own pace. Complete every chapter.

For therapist-client use—Assign one chapter and use it as a springboard for the next therapy session. Go at the adoptee's pace. It is essential that the therapist have a personal copy of the workbook.

For support group use—We suggest assigning one chapter for homework but then letting the group set the pace. It is beneficial for the same leader to facilitate the meetings. See Appendix C for specific instructions.

For parents and kids (ages nine and upward) use—It is recommended that both parent and teen have a workbook and that they set aside a special time for dialogue about the homework. It is important that parents set aside preconceived ideas about how their teen views adoption. Parental perceptions are usually different than the adoptee's. There should be no pressure put on the child/teen to share what is uncomfortable or too personal. Let him/her set the pace.

CONTENTS

PART I
THOUGHTS INDICATING
I MIGHT HAVE BURIED EMOTIONS ABOUT
SEPARATION FROM MY FIRST FAMILY

Under His Wings
WORKBOOK

CHAPTER 1

"I feel like
something's
missing"

The Scripture Base for Moses' Life

Exodus 2: 1-9:

[1] Now a man of the tribe of Levi married a Levite woman, [2] and she became pregnant and gave birth to a son. When she saw that he was a fine child, she hid him for three months. [3] But when she could hide him no longer, she got a papyrus basket for him and coated it with tar and pitch. Then she placed the child in it and put it among the reeds along the bank of the Nile. [4] His sister stood at a distance to see what would happen to him.

[5] Then Pharaoh's daughter went down to the Nile to bathe, and her attendants were walking along the riverbank. She saw the basket among the reeds and sent her female slave to get it. [6] She opened it and saw the baby. He was crying, and she felt sorry for him. "This is one of the Hebrew babies," she said.

[7] Then his sister asked Pharaoh's daughter, "Shall I go and get one of the Hebrew women to nurse the baby for you?" [8] "Yes, go," she answered. So the girl went and got the baby's mother. [9] Pharaoh's daughter said to her, "Take this baby and nurse him for me, and I will pay you." So the woman took the baby and nursed him.

The Story of Moses

Jochebed felt her first labor pain late in the afternoon and by nightfall she had given birth to a beautiful baby boy. It was a bittersweet experience for Jochebed, for death was crouching at her door. Pharaoh, the wicked king of Egypt, in a desperate attempt to keep the Israelites from flourishing and ultimately dethroning him, issued an edict. He ordered Israelite midwives to kill all male Israelite babies at birth. The God-fearing midwives, however, did just the opposite. They welcomed the babies into the world and tenderly placed them at their mothers' breasts. When Pharaoh learned that the midwives were sparing the lives of the Israelite babies, he was furious and commanded that *all* male babies be drowned in the Nile River.

As her baby began to suckle, Jochebed's heart began to race, for she could hear the sound of Egyptian soldiers passing by. How would she ever keep the baby quiet? If the soldiers heard him cry, they would tear down the door and immediately kill him. If only Amram were home. He would know what to do. But he was forced into slave labor laying brick and mortar at Pharaoh's palace. How disappointed he would be to have missed the birth of his son. Knowing that the soldiers lurking outside could seize her baby at any given moment, Jochebed prayed, "Oh, God, please show me a way to save the life of my baby."

As she prayed, the idea of placing him in a protective basket came to mind. "Yes!" she said to God, arms outstretched. "This is what I shall do when the time is right." When she could hide him no longer, she got a papyrus basket and coated it with tar and pitch. Then she placed the child in it and put it among the reeds along the bank of the Nile" (v. 3-4). Miriam, the baby's sister, stood at a distance to see what would happen. About the same time, Pharaoh's daughter, Hatshepsut, went to the Nile to bathe and heard the frantic cry of a baby. "She saw the basket among the reeds and sent her slave girl to get it. She opened it and saw the baby. He was crying, and she felt sorry for him" (v. 5-6).

This concludes the first narrative about Moses. Here are a few questions to help you process the narrative:

1. Why was baby Moses crying? (The root meaning of crying: weep, bewail, sob, weep continually, weep longer and weep bitterly.)

_____

_____

2. Do you think a small baby can remember anything? Why or why not?

_____

_____

3. How do you think Moses felt in the basket? Give descriptor words!

_____

_____

4. Why do you think Hatshepsut (Pharaoh's daughter) felt sorry for Moses? Do you think this is why she adopted him?

_____

_____

5. How do you think Jochebed, Moses' Mother, felt as she placed her baby in the crocodile-infested Nile?

_____

_____

How Moses Saw God

Certainly at a few weeks of age, when Moses was put in the basket in the crocodile-infested Nile, he had no concept of God. Probably all he had were sensory memories (sight, touch, hearing, taste) of what was familiar--the sound of his mother's voice, the sweet breast milk, the sounds of the happy voices in the home where he was born, and the soft breasts from which he nursed.

As he was placed in the basket, all that was familiar disappeared. For the first time in his life, he might have felt like an orphan. He had no awareness of **Jehovah**--the Being who is absolutely Self-Existent, the One who in himself possesses essential life and permanent existence. Even though his mother wasn't there with Moses when he was floating on the Nile, Jehovah was. Jehovah's strong hands were holding him up and keeping him safe. Psalm 63:7-8 says, "Because you are my help, I sing in the shadow of your wings. I stay close to you; your right hand upholds me."

How You See God

Please refer to the list of Names for Jesus in Scripture in Appendix B and list three to five names for God that stand out to you. It will be encouraging to look back when finished with the workbook and see how your perception has grown!

You can record your words here:

_____

_____

How Other Adoptees Feel

(Use a highlighter to remember meaningful quotes!)

> I am adopted! Someone didn't want me. This became my story, my scar and my struggle. When I learned of my adoption, compounded by dynamics in my family life, I 'heard' only that someone DIDN'T want me. I was rejected somewhere and somehow, I was now different. All of this became the energy force that kept me, motivated me and often controlled me on a lifetime course of anger, debate, searching and stubborn determination to prove that 'they,' whoever the natural parents were, were wrong to give me up.
>
> –article for *Jewel among Jewels Adoption News*
> by Dr. Richard Gilbert

1. Have you ever feel like Dr. Gilbert? When?

   _____

   _____

2. Did you realize at some point that someone *didn't* want you…and that to be a "chosen child" meant that you were first relinquished (placed for adoption)? If so, how old were you when you realized this?

   _____

   _____

3. Check the following bulleted comments which ring true for you:
   - ❏ I wake up at night and cry, but I don't know why.
   - ❏ Something inside doesn't feel right.
   - ❏ I am crying on the inside but the tears won't come.
   - ❏ I need my parents to understand that I have an invisible wound.
   - ❏ I need the freedom to cry.
   - ❏ I need comfort.
   - ❏ If I were a diabetic, they would give me insulin. If I were deaf, they would give me hearing aids. Why don't they do anything for my wound from adoption?

Learning about Adoption

What I discovered is what I call the primal wound, a wound which is physical, emotional, psychological and spiritual; a wound which causes pain so profound as to have been described as cellular by those adoptees who allowed themselves to go that deeply into their pain. I began to understand this wound as having been caused by the separation of the child from his biological mother, the connection to whom seems mystical, mysterious, spiritual and everlasting.

> –*The Primal Wound: Understanding the Adopted Child,*
> by Nancy Verrier

The loss inherent in adoption is unlike other losses we have come to expect in a lifetime, such as death or divorce. Adoption is more pervasive, less socially recognized and more profound.

> --*Being Adopted: The Lifelong Search for Self,*
> by David M. Brodzinsky, Ph.D. and Marshall D. Schechter, M.D.

Can a baby under one year 'remember' this traumatic separation from his original parents? No, he will probably not remember these events as a series of pictures which can be recalled. What is remembered, or preserved, is anxiety, a primitive kind of terror, which returns in waves in later life. Loss and danger of loss of love become recurrent themes or life patterns. What is preserved may be a profound moodiness or depression later in life, the somatic memory of the first tragic loss, which returns from the unremembered past even, ironically, at moments of pleasure and success. What is preserved is the violation of trust, of the ordered world of infancy in which love, protection and continuity of experience are invested in people. The arbitrary fate that broke the first human bonds may damage or shatter that trust, so that when love is given again it may not be freely returned. And finally, what is preserved is likely to be a wound to the embryonic personality in the first year which may have profound effects upon later development.

> -- *Every Child's Birthright*, by Selma Fraiberg

Putting My Feelings and Needs into Words

1. How do you feel as you embark on this journey of talking about adoption in-depth? Check the statements with which you agree and explain why you checked them on the lines that follow:

    ☐ I really don't want to be doing this.
    ☐ Adoption is no big deal to me.
    ☐ I am terrified.
    ☐ I am nervous.
    ☐ I doubt this book is going to help me.
    ☐ I am afraid my adoptive parents will be hurt.
    ☐ I feel a fierce loyalty to my adoptive parents and would never do anything to jeopardize our relationship.
    ☐ Great…I love talking about adoption.
    ☐ I look forward to this because I have a need to be with other adoptees and hear their experiences.
    ☐ I am excited about this…I have never had such an opportunity!

    _____

    _____

2. How often was/is adoption discussed in your home?

    _____

    _____

3. When did you learn you were adopted?

    _____

    _____

4. If you could sum up your adoption experience in one word, what would it be?

    _____

5. Describe your perception of being separated from your first family (parents bringing me into their house; baby in a basket, baby in a dumpster, baby on the steps of a church, parents picking baby out, parents so happy when they lay eyes on you, the day you lost your birth mother, etc).

_____

_____

6. Draw a picture illustrating your perception of adoption/foster care/orphanage from question #5 (how you feel as you embark on this journey). Use only your left hand (or right if you are left-handed).

7. How do you think your birth mother felt at your birth?

_____

_____

8. Do you know the circumstances that prompted her decision to place you for adoption? If not, or if so, how does this make you feel?

_____

_____

9. How do you think your adoptive parents felt when they first saw you?

_____

_____

10. Do you ever feel like something's not right inside? You're all mixed up, but can't even explain it? If so, when, where?

11. Do you ever feel like you are crying on the inside, yet tears won't come? If so, how long does the feeling last?

12. What do you need most when you are feeling confused and mixed up inside? List specific ways of getting this need met.

Writing a Letter TO and FROM My Birth Mother

- Write a letter TO your birth mother about the possibility that you were wounded when she disappeared from your life.

- Write a letter to yourself FROM your birth mother, expressing thoughts and feelings you think she would want you to know about her reasons for placing you for adoption and how she feels about what you have just said in your letter to her.

Letters TO and FROM

My Birth Mother

_____

_____
_____
_____
_____
_____
_____
_____
_____
_____
_____
_____
_____
_____
_____
_____
_____
_____
_____
_____
_____

Digging Deep for Answers to My Adoption Questions

1. Read Psalm 91:4... *"He will cover you with his feathers, and under his wings you will find refuge; his faithfulness will be your shield and rampart."* Where are we to seek safety when we have conflicting or anxiety-producing thoughts about our separation from our birth mothers/fathers?

   _____

   _____

2. Read Psalm 139:13... *"For you created my inmost being; you knit me together in my mother's womb."* What does this say about who created you?

   _____

   _____

3. Read Psalm 139:15... *"My frame was not hidden from you when I was made in the secret place, when I was woven together in the depths of the earth."* Were you ever alone?

   _____

   _____

4. Read Psalm 139:16a... *"Your eyes saw my unformed body..."* Who saw your unformed body?

   _____

   _____

5. Read Psalm 139:16b... *"all the days ordained for me were written in your book before one of them came to be."* Who planned every day of your life?

   _____

   _____

6. In light of this Psalm, what conclusions do you draw about yourself?

_____

_____

7. What do Psalms 61:3-4..."*For you have been my refuge, a strong tower against the foe. I long to dwell in your tent forever and take refuge in the shelter of your wings,*" and Psalm 91:4... "*He will cover you with his feathers, and under his wings you will find refuge; his faithfulness will be your shield and rampart,*" mean in practical terms? How does it apply to your life situation right now?

_____

_____

8. If you're not sure about this "wound" resulting from separation from your birth mother, what should you seek more than anything? See John 8:32... "*Then you will know the truth, and the truth will set you free.*"

_____

_____

9. What is the "take away" for you after completing this chapter? How will your life change as a result of your study?

_____

_____

Thoughts, Insights, Goals, and Prayers

Would you be willing to ask God to make himself real to you as you begin this study? If so, record your request. If not, perhaps you could ask God to create a willing heart within you.

_____

_____

Now that we've identified the "core issue" (separation from your birth mother), and the feelings that often accompany it, we'll examine another feeling that often impacts the adoptee's relationship within the adoptive family—feeling like you don't belong.

CHAPTER 2

"I often feel like I don't belong"

The Scripture Base for Moses' Life

Exodus 2:10

[10] When the child grew older, she took him to Pharaoh's daughter and he became her son. She named him Moses, saying, "I drew him out of the water."

The Story of Moses

When Pharaoh's daughter, Hatshepsut, heard the baby's cry, an adoptive mother's heart was born. This was an Israelite baby. A baby her father, Pharoah, wanted dead. What would he say if he learned that she had rescued a baby that he declared must die?

"What great lengths this baby's mother must have gone to in order to save his life," Hatshepsut might have said to herself. The little ark was so carefully sealed that not even a drop of water reached the baby. "What loving hands must have prepared this for him."

Jochebed's daughter, Miriam, watched the events unfold from behind the tall grasses surrounding the Nile. When she saw Hatshepsut's concern about the baby's need for nursing, she approached her saying, "Shall I go and get one of the Hebrew women to nurse the baby for you" (v. 7)?

"Yes, go!" she replied. Miriam rushed to her mother with Hatshepsut close behind. Hatshepsut said to Jochebed, "Take this baby and nurse him for me, and I will pay you" (v. 6-10). Can you imagine the excitement Miriam experienced? She may have been serious on the outside, but smiling on the inside!

Thus, in an incredible turn of events, Jochebed once again held the child she cherished. How good it felt to put his little head on her shoulder and cuddle him! How soft was his skin, how familiar his cry. That Pharoah's daughter, the Pharoah who wanted the baby killed, was the one who snatched him from the jaws of death.

When Moses was old enough to be weaned (around three years of age), his parents prepared to take him to Hatshepsut as the promised. As Jochebed dressed her little boy for the last time, uncontrollable tears flowed. Amram, Moses' father, was in the other room silently rehearsing a child-like explanation of the upcoming event for his son. That night, Amram prayed aloud. *Where should I begin, Father God? How can a three year-old child possibly understand that we are doing this to save his life? What if my son wonders if we are giving him to Hatshepsut because something is wrong with him or because we don't love him?*

The next morning, Amram explained the dreaded event to his son. Moses buried his tear-drenched face in Amram's lap. "No, papa! Me stay here with you and mama!"

In silence, the little family gathered his belongings and walked the dusty road together, hand-in-hand, away from the huts of Israel toward Pharaoh's magnificent palace. The boy clung to Jochebed as they approached the palace doors. Jochebed lifted him up and carried him inside as he tucked his head beneath her chin. *Could it be that our son is really three?*

A servant opened the huge gold-plated palace door and ushered them in. Hatshepsut, dressed in Egyptian finery, met them with arms outstretched. Moses clung to Jochebed, tears streaming down his cheeks,

After a few minutes of exchanging pleasantries, Amram and Jochebed their rehearsed words with quivering lips. *We have to go now, son. You will be staying here with this nice lady. We love you and will never forget you.*

Mama, papa, don't go! Miriam? Aaron?

Even though Jochebed's and Amram's hearts were breaking, they were confident that God had saved their son for a specific role in history—he was adopted for a purpose. And so they left in tears, putting their trust in God.

Moses threw himself on the palace floor, kicking and screaming. Whenever Hatesphut approached, he ran to another place on the floor and repeated the kicking and screaming.

The first thing Hatshepsut did was to give her new son a name. *I named him Moses because I drew him out of the water* (v. 10).

What name did he have in his birth family's home? Surely it must have been a Hebrew name. But now he was to be called by another name--an Egyptian name. Little Moses felt all mixed up inside. If he were able to put his feelings into words he might have said, *I don't feel like I belong to anyone. I don't belong to my adoptive mother or my birth parents.* If you were Moses, how would you have felt when your parents, brother and sister disappear, never to return, behind that huge palace door?

Give specific words that would describe his emotions as well as behavior. Please refer to the Feelings Chart in Appendix A.

How Moses Saw God

Parents model the character of God for their children. Moses had learned to trust his parents to meet every one of his needs. But then they seemingly "gave him" to a person that was a stranger to him. Even though his parents knew this was God's will for their son, he was too young to understand. He felt so terribly alone and would learn later in life that the invisible God was there with him.

Perhaps Moses transferred his this perceived abandonment to God? He had yet to come to know God as **El Shaddai**. "El" means God. "Shaddai" comes from the word "breast" and means the All-Sufficient One, the Pourer or Shedder forth of blessings. El Shaddai was invisibly there with Moses, providing a spiritual breast for Moses' spirit. *"My grace is sufficient for you, for my power is made perfect in weakness"* (II Corinthians 12:9).

How You See God

Please refer to the list of Names for Jesus in Scripture in Appendix B and list three to five names for God that stand out to you. It will be encouraging to look back when finished with the workbook and see how your perception has grown!

You can record your words here:

_____

_____

How Other Adoptees Feel

Check the bulleted statements with which you identify:

- ❏ Even though I knew both my birth and adoptive parents, I felt like I didn't belong anywhere.
- ❏ There was a different role in the family for me as an adoptee.
- ❏ After my reunion with my birth family, I still didn't feel like I belonged anywhere.
- ❏ I felt like a square peg in a round hole in my adoptive family.
- ❏ I have always felt different.
- ❏ I go from group to group, trying to find a place where I fit in, and then when I realize I don't, I conform to the behavior and identity of the group.
- ❏ I used to lay awake at night and wonder why my birth mother didn't keep me.
- ❏ I am afraid of new situations. I need to verbalize the unspeakable feelings I have toward my birth parents for giving me up. Feelings like rage, hate and confusion.
- ❏ I need to be able to share these feelings with my adoptive parents.
- ❏ I need a "safe," non-judgmental person or group with whom I can share my pain.

> Betrayal curls through my soul like a sunken steel mesh that buttresses skyscrapers. I can't quite see it, but it's what I'm built on. It wrinkles my life, and bristles in me in inappropriate ways. All future betrayals found an anchor in that first foundational trauma, and reverberated off the walls of the gaping wound in my soul. What took its place was the stand-in-for-me, the one which would conform and smile and not hurt, who would fit in nicely with the life my adoptive parents constructed for me. And thus, the betrayal continued—my needs were always obscured by their own—but I didn't feel it any more, consciously. I didn't feel much at all. Except that, paradoxically, I felt betrayal everywhere, projected it onto well-meaning but forgetful friends, or bosses just doing their jobs, or lovers simply being human.
>
> --Essay entitled, "Betrayal" by Marcy Wineman Axness, Ph.D., adoptee and founder of Quantam Parenting

Learning about Adoption

Adoptees in particular have many conflicting elements in their lives...an adoptee's amended birth certificate says he was born to one set of parents, and his own parents tell him he was born to another. He was told he was relinquished because his birth mother loved him, yet he knows from experience that he never wants to be far from the people he loves. He hears from some people that he is a chosen child, yet he hears from others that being adopted is not as good as living with your 'real' parents. The search, then, is an attempt to reconcile cognitive dissonance, to bring order out of a sense of chaos.

> --*Being Adopted...The Lifelong Search for Self*,
> David M. Brodzinsky, Ph.D. and Marshall D. Schechter, M.D.

Many adoptees have told me that they find it difficult to believe in a God who allows babies to be separated from their mothers. It violates their sense of order in the universe, replacing order and meaning with chaos and terror. There is a sense of being a mistake, of having no right to exist in the world. There is no sense of belonging in the family into which they were placed, that into which they were born, or in the universal schema.

> --*The Primal Wound: Understanding the Adopted Child*
> Nancy Verrier

Putting My Feelings and Needs into Words

1. Do you ever feel like you don't belong in your adoptive family? Do you feel like a square peg in a round hole? If so, when and where?

   _____

   _____

2. Can you identify situations that trigger those feelings of not belonging? Be specific.

   _____

   _____

3. What do you do when you feel this way? Isolate yourself? Conform to the expectations of others? Describe situations and behaviors.

   _____

   _____

4. Do you think feeling different is the same as feeling like you don't belong? If so, explain.

_____

_____

5. Do you feel betrayed by your birth mother because she placed you for adoption? Explain.

_____

_____

6. Many adoptive parents explain the birth mother's decision to place the baby for adoption by saying, "She did it because she loved you." How does this statement make you feel?"

_____

_____

7. Give your reaction to this statement: "Adoption is the loving option."

_____

_____

8. Have you ever felt betrayed by God because he allowed your life to be touched by adoption? Explain why or why not.

_____

_____

Writing a Letter TO and FROM My Birth Mother

1. Write a letter TO your birth mother, expressing feelings of abandonment, not belonging, or betrayal. What do you want her to know about your feelings, thoughts, and beliefs?

2. Write a letter FROM your birth mother, imagining what she may say in response to your letter.

Letters TO and FROM

My Birth Mother

_____

_____

_____

_____

_____

_____

_____

_____

_____

_____

_____

_____

_____

_____

_____

_____

_____

_____

_____

Digging Deep for Answers to my Adoption Questions

1. Read Psalm 27:10…"Though my father and mother forsake me, the LORD will receive me." What does God promise when our birth parents abandon us?

_____

_____

2. A man in the Bible named Job lost all his family. What impact did this have on his perception of God? Read Job 23:8-9…"But if I go to the east, he is not there; if I go to the west, I do not find him. When he is at work in the north, I do not see him; when he turns to the south, I catch no glimpse of him."

_____

_____

3. How did Job calm himself? See Job 23:10…"But he knows the way that I take; when he has tested me, I will come forth as gold."

_____

_____

4. What is the "take away" for you from this chapter? How will your life change?

_____

_____

Thoughts, Insights, Goals and Prayers

_____

_____

Feeling different in a bad kind of way is nothing more than shame. When you finish this workbook, you will embrace your differences and be able to celebrate who God made you to be. First comes hard work and you're doing great.

The next chapter deals with anger. Anybody have issues with anger? Read on, friend.

Under His Wings
WORKBOOK

CHAPTER 3

"I blow up
easily and
hurt others"

The Scripture Base for Moses' Life

Exodus 2:11-25

[11] One day, after Moses had grown up, he went out to where his own people were and watched them at their hard labor. He saw an Egyptian beating a Hebrew, one of his own people. [12] Looking this way and that and seeing no one, he killed the Egyptian and hid him in the sand. [13] The next day he went out and saw two Hebrews fighting. He asked the one in the wrong, "Why are you hitting your fellow Hebrew?" [14] The man said, "Who made you ruler and judge over us? Are you thinking of killing me as you killed the Egyptian?" Then Moses was afraid and thought, "What I did must have become known." [15] When Pharaoh heard of this, he tried to kill Moses, but Moses fled from Pharaoh and went to live in Midian, where he sat down by a well.

The Story of Moses

Moses is now an adult, quite a puzzling adult, to others as well as himself. Word had it that as a child he had a short fuse. Temper tantrums in the palace were common, accompanied by deep hostility toward Hatshepsut, his adoptive mother. From where did this anger come? And why was his adoptive mother usually the target? One day Moses' anger hit an all-time high when he saw an Egyptian brutally abusing a Hebrew slave. As he watched the man being ruthlessly kicked and beaten, he snuck up from behind and grabbed the Egyptian by the neck. He began punching him mercilessly, first in the face, then in the stomach. Within seconds, the Egyptian was dead. The other Hebrew man who was there fled as Moses looked frantically from left to right, to see if anyone else had witnessed the murder. He fell to the ground, and with sweat running from his brow, he furiously shoveled huge handfuls of sand to make a hole big enough to bury the body. The following day, he intervened in yet another dispute-- this time between two Hebrew men. "What are you arguing about? Can I help?" he might have asked. When one of them asked if he was a self-appointed judge like he had been the day before, adrenaline pumped through Moses' veins as he headed toward the backside of the desert. Perhaps there he would be safe from his life crime-stained life. Perhaps there he could begin life anew.

1. What do you think motivated Moses to become so involved in the two disputes?

_____

_____

2. What do you think was going through his head as he ran to the backside of the desert?

_____

_____

How Moses Saw God

Those who are wounded wound others. Moses was wounded profoundly when he lost his birth family, his heritage and his history. In the years to come, he would come to know **Jehovah-rophe**, the Healer of life's sicknesses and sorrows. Exodus 15: 26b says, "…for I am the Lord, who heals you."

How You See God

Please refer to the list of Names for Jesus in Scripture in Appendix B and list three to five names for God that stand out to you. It will be encouraging to look back when finished with the workbook and see how your perception has grown!

You can record your words here:

_____

_____

How Other Adoptees Feel

Check the statements with which you agree and explain why you checked them on the lines that follow:
- ❏ I am angry at my birth mother—she put me into the arms of a stranger when I had no say in the matter.
- ❏ My anger comes out at the strangest times.
- ❏ I am angry with God for touching my life with adoption. Why did He choose me to suffer like this?
- ❏ I am angry when others treat me like a child—like hospital officials do when I request a copy of my birth record. They say to me in a condescending voice, "Now, dear, are you an adoptee?"
- ❏ I am angry that my birth parents abandoned me. I am angry that I can't have a "normal" birth certificate. I have to have an amended one that removes any record of my history.
- ❏ I can't get hold of the idea that she (my birth mother) is alive and went on with life without me.
- ❏ I need to know that it is permissible for me to be angry with God about my adoption and that he welcomes my anger and is big enough to handle it.
- ❏ I need to know that anger means I am beginning to heal. The part of me that has been shut down is coming to life.

Learning about Adoption

Anger, the other side of depression, is always waiting to be tapped in the adoptee. Anger that adoptees have built up over the years can erupt as uncontrollable rage. There is the unexpressed anger that they are adopted; anger that they are different; anger that they are powerless to know their origins; anger that they cannot express their real feelings in a family climate of denial. When this anger is allowed to build in a child over the years, it will eventually surface as aggression—stealing, setting fires, destroying property—and if left unresolved, as violence.
—*Journey of the Adopted Self*, by Betty Jean Lifton

What are adoptees angry about? Lots of things. They're angry with people like me because we gave them away. They need an explanation or an apology. Of course they can't get one because we're nowhere to be found, which frustrates them and makes them mad as hell. Some are also angry because we sent them away from their 'kind,' abandoning them to an environment in which they suffer chronic, cumulative and vast feelings of unacceptability. They're angry with people like you (adoptive parents) because they can't explore the subject of adoption openly. Why? Because it makes you cringe. They're also angry because you don't understand how they feel, or worse, denigrate their feelings because you can't relate to them…They are also angry because people in general treat adopted people differently: school teachers type-cast them, health-care professionals treat them as medical risks, outsiders consider them inferior by assuming that they are the spawn of people who came 'from the other side of the tracks.
—"The Angry Adoptee" article in *Quest:*
The Newsletter for KinQuest, by Carol Kimissaroff

"Anger is a response to separation…"
—*Separation, Anxiety and Anger*, by John Bowlby

"It's easier to be mad than sad." Gregory C. Keck, Ph.D.

Putting my Feelings and Needs into Words

1. Do you see anger as a significant problem in your life? Do others? Explain.

2. What types of situations provoke your anger?

_____

_____

3. When you were growing up, did you throw temper tantrums? At what age?

_____

_____

4. Can you recognize when you are angry? Do you have physical symptoms that accompany it (sweaty palms, racing heart, dry mouth, etc.)?

_____

_____

5. Were you allowed to express your anger in your adoptive home?

_____

_____

6. How did your parents react when you expressed anger?

_____

_____

7. Has anyone ever given you permission to be angry?

_____

_____

8. Make an "anger list.

_____

_____

9. Have you ever experienced depression (the flip side of anger)? When?

_____

_____

10. What do you do when you are depressed?

_____

_____

11. Has anyone ever celebrated your anger, recognizing it is a necessary step in the healing process?

Who? When?

_____

_____

12. What do you need most when you are angry? After you are angry?

_____

_____

13. What are some healthy ways of managing your anger?

_____

_____

14. What are some options for managing depression?

_____

_____

Writing a Letter TO and FROM My Birth Mother

1. If you are aware of any anger about your birth mother placing you for adoption, write a letter TO her

   expressing it.

   _____

   _____

2. Write a letter FROM your birth mother to you in response to your thoughts.

   _____

   _____

Letters TO and FROM

My Birth Mother

_____

_____

_____

_____

_____

_____

_____

_____

_____

_____

_____

_____

_____

_____

_____

_____

_____

_____

_____

_____

Digging Deep for Answers to my Adoption Questions

1. Read Ephesians 4:26…*"In your anger do not sin:" Do not let the sun go down while you are still angry…´* What does God say about anger?

   _____

   _____

2. Put Ephesians 4:26 in your own words.

   _____

   _____

3. Read Ephesians 4:26-27… *"In your anger do not sin: Do not let the sun go down while you are still angry, and do not give the devil a foothold."* What happens when we don't deal with anger on a daily basis?

   _____

   _____

4. Read Matthew 12:20… *"A bruised reed he will not break, and a smoldering wick he will not snuff out, till he has brought justice through to victory."* What is God's promise to those who are depressed?

   _____

   _____

5. What does God promise to those who are depressed? See Psalm 18:28…*"You, LORD, keep my lamp burning; my God turns my darkness into light."*

   _____

   _____

6. What did Job learn when he felt like he was in the dark? See Job 12:22…*"He reveals the deep things of darkness and brings utter darkness into the light."*

_____

_____

7. What is the "take away" for you this week? How will your life change?

_____

_____

Thoughts, Insights, Goals and Prayers

_____

_____

If we don't deal with the anger resulting from the original adoption wound that we discussed in chapter one, it comes to the surface when we least expect it. Keeping it submerged beneath our consciousness is like trying to keep a beach ball submerged under water. It is impossible! Sooner or later, it pops up! If we keep anger submerged, it turns into depression. Sometimes serious depression. In order to manage painful emotions, many of us fantasize about our birth families. That is a way of escape. We will talk about that next.

Under His Wings
WORKBOOK

CHAPTER 4

"I sometimes fantasize about my birth family"

The Scripture Base for Moses' Life

Exodus 2:16-23

¹⁶ Now a priest of Midian had seven daughters, and they came to draw water and fill the troughs to water their father's flock. ¹⁷ Some shepherds came along and drove them away, but Moses got up and came to their rescue and watered their flock.

¹⁸ When the girls returned to Reuel their father, he asked them, "Why have you returned so early today?"

¹⁹ They answered, "An Egyptian rescued us from the shepherds. He even drew water for us and watered the flock."

²⁰ "And where is he?" Reuel asked his daughters. "Why did you leave him? Invite him to have something to eat."

²¹ Moses agreed to stay with the man, who gave his daughter Zipporah to Moses in marriage. ²² Zipporah gave birth to a son, and Moses named him Gershom, saying, "I have become a foreigner in a foreign land."

²³ During that long period, the king of Egypt died. The Israelites groaned in their slavery and cried out, and their cry for help because of their slavery went up to God. ²⁴ God heard their groaning and he remembered his covenant with Abraham, with Isaac and with Jacob. ²⁵ So God looked on the Israelites and was concerned about them.

The Story of Moses

On his way to the backside of the desert to a place called Midian, Moses met and then married a woman named Zipporah. She bore him a son, and Moses named him Gershom, which means, "I have become an alien in a foreign land" (v. 22).

In this new life as a married man and father, Moses became a shepherd for his father-in-law, Jethro. Needless to say, it was a cultural shock going from a pampered life in a palace to tending sheep in the hills of Midian.

While tending sheep, he could slip away into a state of fantasy. At times he would imagine himself being rescued and loved by a strong, compassionate person. At other times, he envisioned himself as a member of a happy family gathered around the fireside, laughing and singing.

Sooner or later, however, the euphoria from the fantasies turned into disappointment, frustration and anger. Even though the happy family and nurturing person were within sight through fantasy, they were just out of reach in real life.

Moses had no idea that he was subconsciously grieving for the family he lost at adoption. One evening when Moses was deep in thought, bright orange flames illuminated the sky. For the first time in his life, his attention was drawn away from the fantasy to a power greater than his pain.

How Moses Saw God

Moses probably knew only about dead Egyptian gods that he had been taught about in his adoptive home. He had no idea that there was a living God who was drawing him into a personal relationship. He had come face to face with **Jehovah-Shammah**, the God who makes his presence real and felt. "If anyone hears my voice and opens the door, I will come in and eat with him, and him with me" (Revelation 3:20b).

How You See God

Please refer to the list of Names for Jesus in Scripture in Appendix B and list three to five names for God that stand out to you. It will be encouraging to look back when finished with the workbook and see how your perception has grown!

You can record your words here:

_____

_____

How Other Adoptees Feel

My Fantasy
The non-identifying information fact sheet tells me,
as I scan it for the millionth time
for the answers to my questions,
that reading, golf, and water-skiing
were their hobbies.
The irony of it,
for they are mine as well.
Wouldn't it be lovely to share just one
sun-soaked afternoon on the lake
with my knight in shining armor,
and the woman whose face I search for in a crowd?
--Amy van der Vleit, adoptee

I was growing without a foundation—a tree without roots. I felt alienated and as I grew, so did my need to know. I often envisioned my biological father as a princely figure, a charming knight in shining armor who could solve any problem I ever had. As I continued through life, I pushed these thoughts to the back of my consciousness, yet still he found his way into my dreams. In one particularly vivid dream, we were in a peaceful green meadow with tall grass and multi-colored flowers. This is what I envision heaven to be. He was on one side of a small wooden fence, I on the other. I could not distinguish the features on his face, but he was tall and blonde, like an angel.
--Tammy Kling, adoptee

I never thought I would meet him first. I thought it would be her, the beautiful phantom Barbie doll who stole my hidden fantasies and my darkest nightmares. But in the end, it was my biological father who became real first—the shadowy, formless life-giver whom I, as an adopted child, rarely thought of. My defenses wrote him off as a classic gun-and-run teenage father. I assumed he simply would have farmed me out to grandmothers or aunts for raising, had he nabbed custody.

--Tamara Kerrill , adoptee

I have had difficulty bringing my birth mother down to earth. I have loved her and hated her, but she has always lived above the clouds. Everyone's mother initially resides with the gods, but she usually comes down to earth when the weather clears. Repression has a way of keeping the weather inclement. Also, one more reluctantly leaves a goddess if he has never lived with her…we search more for our image of the person we have lost than for the actual person.

--*Second Choice* autobiography by Robert Anderson, M.D., adoptee

"I always liked TV shows oriented toward the ideal family. In fact, I got obsessed with them. I was looking for loving, caring parents that I made up in my mind. I fantasized about my birth mother. She lived in a brick home, but had no face."

--Greg Ebert, adoptee

Check the statements which are most meaningful to you and explain why on the lines that follow:
- ❐ I need to be able to verbalize my fantasies.
- ❐ My deepest fantasy is to be held in my birth mother's arms.
- ❐ I don't know if I have adoption fantasies.
- ❐ I have always feared that my birth mother would be a bag lady.
- ❐ I need to learn that fantasy is a normal aspect of an adoptee's emotional life.
- ❐ I need to know that I need not feel guilty for having adoption fantasies, for without them, the pain would have been unbearable.

Learning about Adoption

Adopted children spend an exorbitant amount of psychic time in fantasy. They may seem to be sitting quietly in their rooms, or just looking out the window, when really they are deep in the Ghost Kingdom imagining scenarios that might have been or still might be…These fantasies are not just the passing fancies with which most people empower themselves at various periods of their lives but actual reality for the adoptee's inner, secret self. They are the mother replacement: the comfort zone that the mother did not provide. They serve the function of the surrogate rag doll that experiential monkeys are given after their real mother has been taken away. They are also a form of grieving, of conjuring up the lost mother, in the same way that children grieving for lost parents are known to conjure up their ghosts. Adoptee fantasies serve a different purpose from those of the non-adopted: they are an attempt to repair one's broken life-narrative, to dream it along.

--*Journey of the Adopted Self* by Betty Jean Lifton

Putting My Feelings and Needs into Words

1. Have you idealized certain men or women (mentors, teachers, priests, rabbis, pastors, parents of friends)?

   _____

   _____

2. What are your expectations for yourself and for others?

   _____

   _____

3. Do you have any repetitive nightmares? If so, describe.

   _____

   _____

4. Do people tend to disappoint you? When? How?

   _____

   _____

5. Are you ever so deep in thought that you miss turns while you are driving? If so, describe.

   _____

   _____

6. Is there anyone with whom you feel comfortable sharing your fantasies? If not, who would be a possibility?

   _____

   _____

7. Many adoptees say that their deepest fantasy is to be held in their birth mothers' arms. Do you identify with this? If so, how do you think it would be? If not, what *is* your deepest adoption fantasy?

   _____

   _____

8. Draw a picture with your left hand of what you think it would be like to have never been adopted and to have grown up with your birth family. Then explain it to the person you are working through this workbook with, if you feel comfortable doing so.

Writing a Letter TO and FROM my Birth Mother

- Write a letter TO your birth mother, describing fantasies (dreams) about what she is like.

- Write a letter of response FROM your birth mother, revealing what you think her deepest fantasies would be about you and how you think she would respond to your fantasies about her.

Letters TO and FROM

My Birth Mother

_____

_____
_____
_____
_____
_____
_____
_____
_____
_____
_____
_____
_____
_____
_____
_____
_____

Digging Deep for Answers to my Adoption Questions

1. Read Philippians 4:19..."*And my God will meet all your needs according to the riches of his glory in Christ Jesus.*" What does God promise to do with the gaping hole in your heart that causes you to fantasize?

   _____

   _____

2. What does God promise will happen if you trust him to heal you from the need to have adoption fantasies? See Psalm 22:5..."To you they cried out and were saved; in you they trusted and were not put to shame."

   _____

   _____

3. How will your life change this week as a result of working through this chapter?

   _____

   _____

Thoughts, Insights, Goals and Prayers

_____

_____

_____

_____

As adoptees, we need not be ashamed of the adoption fantasies we have entertained about the perfect family or parent. They were God's gift to keep us safe from unbearable pain until we were ready to deal with it. Because we may have spent time fantasizing, we can become confused about our identity. We'll talk about that next.

Under His Wings
WORKBOOK

CHAPTER 5

"I am confused about my identity"

The Scripture Base for Moses' Life

Exodus 3:1-6

[1] Now Moses was tending the flock of Jethro his father-in-law, the priest of Midian, and he led the flock to the far side of the wilderness and came to Horeb, the mountain of God. [2] There the angel of the LORD appeared to him in flames of fire from within a bush. Moses saw that though the bush was on fire it did not burn up. [3] So Moses thought, "I will go over and see this strange sight—why the bush does not burn up." [4] When the LORD saw that he had gone over to look, God called to him from within the bush, "Moses! Moses!" And Moses said, "Here I am." [5] "Do not come any closer," God said. "Take off your sandals, for the place where you are standing is holy ground." [6] Then he said, "I am the God of your father, the God of Abraham, the God of Isaac and the God of Jacob." At this, Moses hid his face, because he was afraid to look at God.

The Story of Moses

One lonely night when Moses was tending the flock of Jethro, his father-in-law, he led the sheep to the far side of the desert and came to the mountain of God. All of a sudden, a blazing light broke the darkness. "There the angel of the Lord appeared to him in flames of fire from within a blazing bush" (3:2).

Moses stopped dead in his tracks with his eyes fixed on the burning bush. "Why is it so bright? Why doesn't the scraggly little thing burn up? Why don't the shooting flames extinguish?" he may have asked himself.

"I will go over and see this strange sight—why the bush does not burn up" Moses said to himself (v. 3). When the Lord saw that he was coming to check it out, he called to him from within the bush, "Moses. Moses"(v. 4)! "Here I am," Moses said, wondering where the voice was coming from (v. 4b). "Do not come any closer. Take off your sandals, for the place you are standing is holy ground" (v. 5). "Holy ground?" Moses may have said, furrowing his brows. "WHAT is holy ground?" "I am the God of your father, the God of Abraham, the God of Isaac and the God of Jacob" (v. 6).

"The God of my father?" Moses may have said. "Which father? My birth father or my adoptive father? I get so confused whenever family heritage is discussed."

"When I was young," he may have thought, "my birth parents probably taught me about the God of Israel, but my adoptive mother taught me about the Egyptian gods. I am so confused."

1. Do you think Moses had any idea that God was involved in his adoption?

   _____

   _____

2. When the voice said, "I am the God of your father," do you think he was aware of a God who

   was alive and who spoke to individuals?

   _____

   _____

41

How Moses Saw God

Moses had yet to learn about **El-Olam**, God of eternity, or God, the Everlasting One. His sovereignty extends through the passing of time and beyond our ability to see or understand. Moses would have to learn to trust in God's sovereign plan in allowing his life to be touched by adoption.

How You See God

Please refer to the list of Names for Jesus in Scripture in Appendix B and list three to five names for God that stand out to you. It will be encouraging to look back when finished with the workbook and see how your perception has grown!

You can record your words here:

_____

_____

How Other Adoptees Feel

Check the statements which are most meaningful to you and explain why on the lines that follow:

❏   When others ask about my nationality, I am so embarrassed. I don't even know what it is.

❏   Before my adoptive parents died they told me that I would inherit all that they had. I didn't even want it. It didn't seem like it was mine.

❏   I absolutely hate it when our class is asked to do a family tree assignment. My family tree has no pattern. It would have to be two trees instead of one.

❏   When our class is asked to bring an ethnic dish to pass, I feel like I can't bring anything.

❏   Who are my *real* parents?

❏   I feel like an alien.

❏   None of the above.

_____

_____

Learning about Adoption

> One night at a dinner party I listened as my host mused about his children: his son looks like his grandfather, but does not have his disposition; his first daughter has his reserved and deep nature; his second daughter looks like his wife's brother and shares his interest in science. Without being conscious of it, he was telling me how his children are connected to the family. Adopted children never hear their parents make such conversation. They don't know who they resemble or who resembles them, whose interests and talents they share. They suffer from what is called 'genealogical bewilderment'—a lack of knowledge of one's real parents and ancestors.
>
> *--Journey of the Adopted Self* by Betty Jean Lifton

Putting my Feelings and Needs into Words

1. Do you ever feel like an "alien?" Like you weren't really born, but were just dropped into your adoptive family? Explain.

   _____

   _____

2. How does it feel not to share looks or personality with your adoptive family?

   _____

   _____

3. If you were asked to draw your family tree, how would you do it? Draw it below:

   How did you feel when drawing the family tree?

   _____

   _____

4. Do you believe you have a "dual identity" because you were adopted? If so, how will you get a true sense of who you really are?

   _____

   _____

Writing a Letter TO and FROM My Birth Mother

- Write a letter TO your birth mother about your confusion about your identity, if you struggle with this. If not, write her about what stood out to you in this chapter.

- Write a letter FROM your birth mother, expressing feelings and thoughts she may want to convey to you.

Under His Wings
WORKBOOK

Letters TO and FROM

My Birth Mother

Digging Deep for Answers to My Adoption Questions

1. Read Romans 8:28-29…*"And we know that in all things God works for the good of those who love him, who have been called according to his purpose. For those God foreknew he also predestined to be conformed to the image of his Son, that he might be the firstborn among many brothers and sisters."* What does God promise to do in and through the confusing things of life for those who belong to him?

   _____

   _____

2. Read Romans 11:17…*"If some of the branches have been broken off, and you, though a wild olive shoot, have been grafted in among the others and now share in the nourishing sap from the olive root."* How could you liken this verse to adoption? Who is the wild olive shoot?

   _____

   _____

3. What does this verse say happened to you? What specific word describes the shoot's relationship to the tree (hint: it starts with "g")?

   _____

   _____

4. With application to adoption, what does the olive shoot receive from the root? Who do you think the root is and what does the shoot receive from it?

   _____

   _____

5. What does God promise you will become? See Isaiah 61:3b…*"They will be called oaks of righteousness, a planting of the LORD for the display of his splendor."*

   _____

   _____

6. What is the "take away" from this chapter? How will your life change?

   _____

   _____

Thoughts, Insights, Goals and Prayers

_____

_____

Our confusion about our identity often results in a drive to be perfect. We will talk about that next.

Under His Wings
WORKBOOK

CHAPTER 6

"I push myself to be perfect"

The Scripture Base for Moses' Life

Exodus 3:4-6

[4] When the LORD saw that he had gone over to look, God called to him from within the bush, "Moses! Moses!" And Moses said, "Here I am." [5] "Do not come any closer," God said. "Take off your sandals, for the place where you are standing is holy ground." [6] Then he said, "I am the God of your father, the God of Abraham, the God of Isaac and the God of Jacob." At this, Moses hid his face, because he was afraid to look at God.

The Story of Moses

"Since this God knows my nationality and my name, what else does he know about me?" Moses might have thought. "Does he know that I killed an Egyptian and buried him in the sand? I have done all I could do to make up for that. I have tried to live a good life. I have literally driven myself to be the best shepherd, father and husband possible."

This was the perfection Moses sought and this was the "persona" he projected to everyone he knew. However, in spite of all his efforts, Moses had a pervasive feeling that he was never doing well enough or being good enough. This was the part of his personality he guarded with his life. This was the real Moses. The accompanying emotions were so intense that he felt like running away. Rage. Resentment. Fear. Anxiety.

1. Do you think Moses was aware that he behaved in ways that weren't in line with who he really was? That he acted the opposite of how he felt on the inside?

   _____

   _____

2. Do you think Moses thought he had to be perfect before God would accept him and use him?

   _____

   _____

How Moses Saw God

Moses was getting to know God as **El-Roi**--the God who sees all. He had yet to learn that the God that sees all looks through a lens of mercy.

How You See God

Please refer to the list of Names for Jesus in Scripture in Appendix B and list three to five names for God that stand out to you. It will be encouraging to look back when finished with the workbook and see how your perception has grown!

You can record your words here:

_____

_____

How Other Adoptees Feel

Check the statements with which you agree and explain why you checked them on the lines that follow:

- ☐ I have mile-high walls of defenses.
- ☐ I try to do everything perfectly so that others won't reject me.
- ☐ My repressed emotions are so powerful that whenever I get close to accessing them in therapy, I shut down.
- ☐ Others have trouble "reading me."
- ☐ I am the greatest actor/actress in the world.
- ☐ I became super-wife, super-mom and super-woman to keep my pain at bay.
- ☐ I have gone through life at the speed of a shining bullet.
- ☐ I ought to do better.
- ☐ I am never pleased with myself.
- ☐ I followed the path of "the good adopted son."
- ☐ I need to know that God has a plan for my life—that I have a role to play in history.

_____

_____

Learning about Adoption

What are *Super You* and *Real You*? *Super You* is a false idealized image you think you have to be in order to be loved and accepted. *Super You* is an imaginary picture of yourself. Since you have been programmed to believe that no one will love you if he gets to know the real you, you strive to become *Super You*, to gain love and acceptance. This distortion extends even to God, who is Absolute Perfection, who demands perfection, and to whom you must somehow present only your good side. You must let God see only *Super You*, not *Real You*."
> --*Healing for Damaged Emotions* by David Seamands

While inside I struggled, outside I strained to present a status-quo face. I wore J. Crew, cooked nutritious meals, went to Mommy and Me, clenched my teeth, and tried to keep it together. I was living what Clarissa Pinkola Estes calls 'the grinning depression.'
> --*"Many Hands: An Adoptee's Healing Journey,"*
> in *Roots & Wings* magazine by Marcy Axness

I was an NFL player, tough and mean, built up like a marble statue, cavalier and confident, a man's man. I guess I was those things, but at the same time, of course, I was still the boy who would cry himself to sleep over the tragic ending of a book.
> -- *A Man and His Mother: An ADOPTED Son's Search*
> by Tim Green, Fox-TV Sports host and best-selling author

Putting my Feelings and Needs into Words

1. Do you think God loves imperfect people? Why or why not?

   _____

   _____

2. Do you condemn yourself for no reason? Explain.

   _____

   _____

3. Are you willing to ask God if he has a special plan for your life?

   _____

   _____

4. Do you dread condemnation from God? If so, for what?

   _____

   _____

5. Do you compare yourself to others? If so, who and when?

_____

_____

6. Do you project an "I-have-it-all-together" image to others, yet feel depressed inwardly? Explain.

_____

_____

7. List some of the ways you project yourself as having it "all together."

_____

_____

8. Are you depressed on the inside but grinning on the outside?

_____

_____

Writing a Letter TO and FROM My Birth Mother

- Write a letter TO your birth mother about your need to be perfect.

- Write a letter FROM your birth mother as she discovers your need to hide your true feelings.

Under His Wings
WORKBOOK

Letters TO and FROM

My Birth Mother

_____

_____

_____

_____

_____

_____

_____

_____

_____

_____

_____

_____

_____

_____

_____

_____

_____

_____

_____

_____

Digging Deep for Answers to My Adoption Questions

1. What does God desire from you? See Psalm 51:6 for your answer.

    _____

    _____

2. What does the Bible say about comparing ourselves to others? See II Corinthians 10:12-13, 17-18.

    _____

    _____

3. Read Romans 5:8. When did God show his love for you the very most?

    _____

    _____

4. With your left hand, draw of picture of Real You and Super You.

5. What life-transforming truth have you learned this week and how will it make a difference in the days ahead?

    _____

    _____

Thoughts, Insights, Goals and Prayers

_____

_____

As adoptees, we may succeed at times by presenting a confident, picture-perfect life to others. However, beneath the veneer of perfectionism is a strong fear of rejection. We will talk about that next.

Under His Wings
WORKBOOK

CHAPTER 7

"I am terrified
of rejection"

The Story of Moses

Exodus 3
Since God had seen every part of Moses, he fully expected God's bar of justice to come down on him hard. It seemed certain to Moses that God would declare him guilty for killing the Egyptian and therefore worthy only of rejection.

This fear of rejection came from the primal wound of separation from Moses' birth mother. No matter how loving the adoption plan, the disappearance of the birth mother translates to the baby as rejection. The infant carries this into all of life's relationships. Moses' fear of rejection also came from guilt—true guilt, for Moses truly had sinned when he murdered the Egyptian. In fact, he pursued a sinful lifestyle because he hadn't loved God with his whole being every moment of every day.

Much to Moses' surprise, God revealed a specific plan for his life. A plan that would relieve the suffering of the Israelites and give them freedom. "So now, go. I am sending you to Pharaoh to bring my people, the Israelites, out of Egypt" (v. 10).
"*Could* it be? Could it *really* be that God *could* and *would* use me to help accomplish his will?" Moses may have said to himself.

All of a sudden Moses' mind flooded with fear.

Have you ever wondered if the reason your birth mother relinquished you was because you were a bad baby? Explain.

How Moses Saw God

Moses may have thought that God was "the big fly swatter in the sky," knocking you down whenever you do wrong." Moses had an incredibly guilty conscience. More than anything, he needed forgiveness for his sins. Moses couldn't provide it for himself. If it were possible, he would have done it long ago. He had come into the presence of **Jehovah-Jireh**, which means, "The Lord will provide." It is a testimony to God's deliverance from sin. What Moses didn't know was that God required that the blood of an unblemished lamb be shed for the forgiveness of sins. The sinner would slay the lamb, take it to the high priest, who would then take it into the tabernacle and ask forgiveness from God. Years after Moses died, God himself, in the Person of his Son, became the Lamb of God that takes away the sin of the world. "The next day John saw Jesus coming toward him and said, 'Look, the Lamb of God, who takes away the sin of the world" (John 1: 29)!

How You See God

Please refer to the list of Names for Jesus in Scripture in Appendix B and list three to five names for God that stand out to you. It will be encouraging to look back when finished with the workbook and see how your perception has grown!

You can record your words here:

_____

_____

Learning about Adoption

Robert S. McGee, Pat Springle and Jim Craddock write in *Your Parents and You*, "For better or for worse, parents represent God to their children. A child's emotional and spiritual foundations are to be provided by them. Most of all, parents are to model the love and strength of God to their children. They are responsible for portraying his reliability, his unconditional love, his acceptance and his purposeful discipline."

Putting My Feelings and Needs Into Words

1. Do you "read" rejection into circumstances and relationships when there is none intended? (Example: a closed door for a part in a play, an unanswered telephone call or letter, your mail icon on your computer indicates you have no mail.) Name specific circumstances when this has occurred.

    _____

    _____

2. What would you feel like if you, like Moses, met God personally? Would you feel guilty or peaceful? Why?

    _____

    _____

3. Do you ever reject others before they can reject you? If so, give examples.

    _____

    _____

Writing a Letter TO and FROM My Birth Mother

*   Write a letter TO your birth mother about your fear of rejection, if you struggle with this. If not, write her about what was meaningful to you in this chapter.

*   Write a letter FROM your birth mother, expressing feelings and thoughts you believe she may want to convey to you.

Under His Wings
WORKBOOK

Letters TO and FROM My Birth Mother

_____

_____

_____

_____

_____

_____

_____

_____

_____

_____

_____

_____

_____

_____

_____

_____

_____

_____

_____

_____

_____

_____

Digging Deep for Answers to my Adoption Questions

1. Read John 1:11. Who in this verse experienced rejection from family? How does this make you feel?

   _____

   _____

2. What is the antidote to the fear of rejection and the need to be perfect? See I John 4:18.

   _____

   _____

3. Where can you find this antidote? See Jeremiah 31:3.

   _____

   _____

4. Read Isaiah 41:9-10. What is the message adoptees need to hear when afraid of rejection?

   _____

   _____

5. What is the "take away" from this chapter? How will your life change?

   _____

   _____

Thoughts, Insights, Goals and Prayers

_____

_____

A close companion of the fear of rejection is a struggle with self-esteem. We will cover that topic next.

CHAPTER 8

"I struggle with self-esteem"

The Story of Moses

Exodus 3-5

Moses was becoming painfully aware of his vulnerability. When God revealed his life calling, Moses thought of every excuse in the book why he shouldn't take the job.

Lack of self-esteem was the first. "Who am I, that I should go to Pharaoh and bring the Israelites out of Egypt" (3:11)?

God answered by giving a promise: "I will be with you" (3:12).

Excuse number two was that he had no message. Nothing to say. "Suppose I go to the Israelites and say to them, 'The God of your fathers has sent me to you,' and they ask me, 'What is his name?' Then what shall I tell them" (3: 13)?

God answered by giving him a message. "I am who I am. This is what you are to tell the Israelites: 'I AM has sent me to you'" (3:14).

Next Moses tried the "no authority" line. "Well, what if they don't believe me or listen to me and say, 'The Lord did not appear to you'" (4:1)?
God countered, "What is that in your hand" (4: 2)?
"A staff," Moses replied.
"What does that have to do with anything?" Moses might have wondered.

The Lord said, "Throw it on the ground" (4: 3).
So Moses threw it on the ground and it became a hissing snake. Moses jumped back in sheer terror.

"Reach out your hand and take it by the tail," God said.
"You've got to be kidding! Pick up a snake by the tail?" Moses was probably thinking. "Nevertheless, Moses reached out and took hold of the snake's tail and it immediately turned back into a staff in his hand" (4:1-4).

Then came excuse number three—I'm not a public speaker! "I have never been eloquent, neither in the past nor since you have spoken to your servant. I am slow of speech and tongue" (4:10).
God replied with questions about creation and then gave a tender promise. "Who gave man his mouth? Who makes him deaf or dumb: Who gives him sight or makes him blind? Is it not I, the Lord? Now go; I will help you speak and will teach you what to say" (4: 13).

"I'm just a big chicken, Lord," Moses might have thought. "… *please* send someone else" (4:13, emphasis mine).

At that point, God stopped nudging Moses toward his life calling. But he didn't give up on him. Instead, he tried "plan B."

"What about your brother, Aaron, the Levite? I know he can speak well. Aaron will be your spokesman before Pharaoh" (5:14).

"Whew!" Moses must have muttered beneath his breath. But then he thought, "My brother? I hardly remember him. He is just a shadowy figure from my past. I am relieved that somebody else is going to do the job, but why did God reach way back into my past and choose somebody from my birth family to do it? I am terrified that Aaron will reject me."

"He is already on his way to meet you, and his heart will be glad when he sees you," God said (4:14).

1. Do you think Moses believed God? What might his thoughts have been?

   _____

   _____

2. Out of all the promises that God gave to Moses in the account you just read, which do you think hit the core issue for him as an adoptee?

   _____

   _____

How Moses Saw God

Moses needed to learn that God was **Jehovah-tsidkenu**—the One who is righteous and the source of *true* acceptance. He needed to learn as Paul did in Philippians 3: 7-9 (*The Message*), "All the things I thought were important are gone from my life compared to the high privilege of knowing Christ Jesus as my Master, first-hand, everything I once thought I had going for me is insignificant—dog dung. I've dumped it all in the trash so that I could embrace Christ and be embraced by him. I didn't want some petty, inferior brand of righteousness that comes from keeping a list of rules when I could get the robust kind that comes from trusting Christ—God's righteousness."

The staff was symbolic of Moses' life. God was asking him to let go of it—to give complete control to him. When Moses picked it up, it was no longer his life but the very life of God.

How You See God

Please refer to the list of Names for Jesus in Scripture in Appendix B and list three to five names for God that stand out to you. It will be encouraging to look back when finished with the workbook and see how your perception has grown!

You can record your words here:

_____

_____

How Other Adoptees Feel

Check the statements with which you agree:
- ❐ I hate being in the limelight.
- ❐ I feel like a loser most of the time.
- ❐ I avoid leadership positions with a passion.
- ❐ I have a deep need to justify myself.
- ❐ Sometimes I pretend I am someone else.
- ❐ I am loyal to others to a fault, even when I am being mistreated.
- ❐ I feel so insecure.
- ❐ I look at others and wish I could be confident like them.
- ❐ I cringe at the words "illegitimate" and "bastard."
- ❐ I feel like damaged goods.
- ❐ I need to learn to trust God—to give him complete control of my life.
- ❐ I need God's assurance that searching for my lost family is acceptable and possibly beneficial.
- ❐ I need to learn God's opinion of me.
- ❐ I need God's acceptance.

Describe the circumstances when these thoughts and feelings are triggered on the lines below:

_____
_____
_____
_____
_____
_____

Learning about Adoption

Nancy Verrier writes in *The Primal Wound*: *Understanding the Adopted Child*, "Distrust is evident, not only in the permanency of relationships, but in the goodness of self…This lack of self-esteem or self-worth is intricately intertwined with the lack of trust and fear of intimacy described by many adoptees with whom I have spoken. I guess it was best summed up by Denise, who said, 'If my own mother couldn't love me, who can?' Reassuring her that her mother did love her isn't helpful because it brings up the non sequitur: 'Your mother really loved you, so she gave you up.' This may make sense to the adult adoptee on the intellectual level, but it doesn't make any sense at all to the baby who resides within that adult."

Putting my Feelings and Needs into Words

1. Do you struggle with self-esteem issues? How and when?

_____
_____

2. Do you ever wish or pretend you were someone else? If so, who and when?

_____
_____

3. How do you feel about being in the limelight and taking on leadership?

_____

_____

4. What do you think God's opinion is of you?

_____

_____

5. Do you ever "sabotage yourself?" In other words, do you back out of commitments when something good is going to happen or when you see that you may be successful? If so, what do you think is the belief driving the withdrawal?

_____

_____

Digging Deep for Answers to My Adoption Questions

1. Look up God's answers to Moses' inadequacies in your Bible:

   a. "I'm not able." Philippians 4:13

   _____

   _____

   b. "I have nothing to say." I Corinthians 15: 3-4

   _____

   _____

   c. "I have no authority." Matthew 28:18-20

   _____

   _____

   d. "I'm not a public speaker." Philippians 2:13

   _____

   _____

   e. "I'm chicken!" Philippians 2:13

   _____

   _____

2. Ezekiel 16: 4-7 (Living Bible) says, "On the day when you were born, you were dumped out into a field and left to die, unwanted—But I [God] came by and saw you there, covered with your own blood, and I said, 'Live! Thrive live a plant in the field.' And you did! You grew up and became—a jewel among jewels." Based on this verse, where was God when you were born? How does this make you feel?

_____

_____

3. What did he say to you? What does the word "live" mean to you?

_____

_____

4. What is God's opinion of you? How does this make you feel?

_____

_____

5. Based on this verse, who is the only one who can heal your lack of self-esteem?

_____

_____

6. Draw a picture, illustrating your worth in God's eyes as a jewel among jewels.

Writing a Letter TO and FROM My Birth Mother

- Write a letter TO your birth mother, telling her about your level of self-esteem at different ages of your life. If you think her relinquishment of you contributed to it, tell her about it.

- Write a letter FROM your birth mother, expressing what you believe her response would be to your thoughts.

Letters TO and FROM

My Birth Mother

How will your life change this week? What is your action step?

_____

_____

_____

_____

_____

Thoughts, Insights, Goals and Prayers

_____

_____

_____

_____

_____

Just like Moses, until we yield control of our lives to Jesus Christ, it is impossible to see ourselves through God's eyes. Try as we may, we will never see our worth through accomplishments or the opinions of others. Moses finally yielded his life to God; therefore he was ready to face his greatest fear--a reunion with his birth brother, Aaron. We will talk about the thoughts and emotions that accompany such a reunion in the next chapter.

Under His Wings
WORKBOOK

CHAPTER 9

"I get uptight
whenever I
think about
a reunion
with my
birth family"

The Story of Moses

Exodus 4

Like many adoptees, Moses probably experienced a tremendous amount of anxiety prior to his reunion with his birth brother, Aaron. "What will I say?" "How will I act?" "Will I laugh or cry?" he may have wondered.

As with all adoption reunions, there is joy as well as pain, blessing as well as a sense of loss. Moses' reunion with Aaron was probably no exception.
As he crossed the desert and neared the mountain of God, how his heart must have skipped! Flashbacks of his traumatic adoption day may have occurred or warm memories of his big brother taking care of him when he was a small child.

As he neared the mountain of God, a tall, slim figure gradually came into view.

"Moses!" Aaron shouted, running toward him, arms outstretched.

"It's so wonderful to see you!" they echoed, kissing one another, first on one cheek and then the other.

"Do you remember when we used to play together when you were little?" Aaron might have asked as they sat by the fireside that evening. "How are mother and father?" Moses probably said. "Are they still living?"

As they talked, Moses experienced feelings he had never known before. Feelings of completeness. Of peace. Of connection.

"Then Moses told Aaron everything the Lord had sent him to say, and also about the miraculous signs he had commanded him to perform" (v. 27-28).

Following this sweet time of fellowship with his long-lost brother, Moses returned to his father-in-law, Jethro, expressing his desire to return to Egypt to see if his people, the Israelites (which included his birth family) were still alive.

One can't help but wonder if a dual-theme began at this point in Moses' life, where his life calling became intricately woven together with his adoption experiences. Not only was he to fulfill the divine command by demanding that Pharaoh release the Israelites, but in a personal, adoption-related way, he was about to face his cruel adoptive grandfather, Pharaoh.

What terror must have filled his heart! He was being stretched reluctantly into a leadership role that would require that he face his greatest fears—rejection by Pharaoh and rejection by the people he would be leading,

God warned that when Aaron demanded release of the Israelites, Pharaoh would refuse to listen ten times. The result would be specific plagues upon the Egyptians. Water would change into blood. Frogs. Gnats. Flies. The livestock would be plagued. Boils. Hail. Locusts. Darkness. The Passover. The death of the firstborn.

Moses watched as Aaron spoke to Pharaoh eight times, but on the ninth confrontation, during the plague of darkness, Moses spoke alone before Pharaoh.

How interesting. It is often in our darkest hours that we embrace God's strength and grace. Moses was proving that those with the deepest fears have the greatest capacity for faith. *Finally*, he was living out his life calling!

1. Do you think the initial conversation between Aaron and Moses was spontaneous, or did it feel a little awkward? Explain.

   _____

   _____

2. How do you think Moses turned his fears into faith?

   _____

   _____

3. How do you think it felt for Moses to hold his own flesh-and-blood relative in his arms and to see someone who probably resembled him physically?

   _____

   _____

How Moses Saw God

Moses was getting to know God as **Jehovah-Rohi**, his Shepherd. Like a shepherd, God would feed and lead Moses as he led the people of Israel. "I will be with you," God said earlier. What music that must have been to Moses' ears! He took this promise by faith and thus was able to step confidently into his life purpose. "He tends his flock like a shepherd: He gathers the lambs in his arms and carries them close to his heart; he gently leads those that have young" (Isaiah 40: 11).

How You See God

Please refer to the list of Names for Jesus in Scripture in Appendix B and list three to five names for God that stand out to you. It will be encouraging to look back when finished with the workbook and see how your perception has grown!

You can record your words here:

_____

_____

How Other Adoptees Feel

Check the statements with which you most agree and explain why on the lines that follow:

- ❏ When I found out my birth mother's name and phone number, I was terrified.
- ❏ I need a break from adoption stuff. I am overwhelmed.
- ❏ I often wonder if my birth parents are alive.
- ❏ I am afraid to tell my adoptive parents about my desire to search.
- ❏ I am afraid that I might seem disloyal to my adoptive parents and I don't want to hurt them.
- ❏ I know my adoptive parents would be so upset by my desire to search that I would have to "protect" them…. take care of them emotionally.
- ❏ The closer I get to the feelings surrounding my past, the faster I run from them.
- ❏ I don't know what I would do if I were rejected at my reunion. I am afraid it would destroy me.
- ❏ I need someone to "hold my feet to the fire" so that I won't avoid my past.
- ❏ I need to prepare myself for possible opposition and rejection at reunion.
- ❏ I need to be reminded often that no matter what the outcome of my search, I will grow.

_____

_____

_____

_____

1. How do you feel when you realize that other adoptees have feelings similar to yours?

_____

_____

2. How have significant people in your life reacted when you expressed the desire to search for your birth family?

_____

_____

3. If you haven't expressed a desire to reunite, how do you imagine they would respond? Check whatever applies from the following:

- ❏ Why open THAT can of worms?
- ❏ That is such an important piece of your life. I understand why you would want to search for your birth family.
- ❏ I always thought there would be a time for this. Go for it!
- ❏ Let by-gones be by-gones.
- ❏ You're asking for trouble.
- ❏ You know who you are in Christ…that is all you need to know.
- ❏ A quivering lip.
- ❏ I will support you in every way possible.

Learning about Adoption

Jayne Schooler writes in *Searching for A Past: The Adopted Adult's Unique Process of Finding Identity*, "Denial or rejection stands as the greatest fear for any adopted person who makes the decision to search. Rejection is an opposing response to a shaky, uncertain extended hand. Rejection is the dashing of hope to embrace and be embraced, to love and to be loved by the one person who has existed only within the deep recesses of the heart."

1. Have you forced yourself not to think about your birth family (denial) as well as a possible reunion with them? If so, how?

2. How would you deal with the pain if your birth relative rejected you? Have you counted the cost?

3. What are some practical ways in which you could prepare yourself for a possible search?

Putting my Feelings and Needs into Words

1. How do you think it would feel to hear your birth mother's voice for the first time?

2. With your left hand, draw the faces of your birth mother and you. (On your day of birth as well as now).

3. Have you learned the art of being gentle with yourself while contemplating reunion—to rest when you feel overwhelmed? What do you do to calm yourself? If you don't know how to take care of yourself, what are some first steps?

4. Do you ever feel guilt when contemplating a reunion, fearing God may not approve? If so, explain.

5. What are your needs as you contemplate reunion or facing repressed thoughts and emotions about your birth family?

6. What do you believe a reunion with birth relatives would do for you? What would you hope to have, if anything, after the reunion that you don't have now?

_____

_____

7. How do you feel when you realize that other adoptees have similar feelings?

_____

_____

Writing Letters TO and FROM My Birth Mother, My Adoptive Mother, and God

- Write a letter TO your birth mother, telling her your feelings about meeting her.

- Write a letter FROM your birth mother, expressing how she would respond to your letter.

- Write a letter TO your adoptive mother, expressing your desires (if you have them) about reunion with your birth relatives. If you have no desire to meet them, tell her why.

- Write a letter FROM your adoptive mother, expressing how you imagine her feelings would be about a possible reunion. Then write what you believe she would tell you after you disclose your desire.

- Write a letter TO God, telling him how you feel about facing your greatest fear.

- Write a letter FROM God, expressing his thoughts toward you at this time.

Letters TO and FROM
My Birth Mother

Letters TO and FROM
My Adoptive Mother

_____

_____

_____

_____

_____

_____

_____

_____

_____

_____

_____

_____

_____

_____

_____

_____

_____

_____

_____

_____

Letters TO and FROM God

_____

_____

_____

_____

_____

_____

_____

_____

_____

_____

_____

_____

_____

_____

_____

_____

_____

_____

_____

_____

Digging Deep for Answers to my Adoption Questions

1. Look up Ecclesiastes 3:1, 6. What does the Bible say about searching?

   _____

   _____

2. Whom should we seek more than anyone? See Luke 12: 31.

   _____

   _____

3. Look up Proverbs 3: 5-6. What part are you to play in your adoption search and what is God's promise if you do?

   _____

   _____

4. What does "acknowledging God in all your ways" mean to you? Check what you believe is true:
   - ☐ Pray for direction.
   - ☐ Ask him to help me learn how he works in my life.
   - ☐ Ask him to make himself real to me.
   - ☐ Ask him to either increase the desire for searching or take it away.
   - ☐ Ask other Christians to pray for me.

5. What does the above verse mean when it says, "And he will make your paths straight?" Cross out what you believe is incorrect:
   - ☐ I'll find my birth parents right away.
   - ☐ God will comfort me with his Holy Spirit.
   - ☐ I won't have any setbacks or frustrations.
   - ☐ I won't experience any conflicting emotions (happy yet scared).
   - ☐ God will make everything peachy.
   - ☐ God will be with me every step of the way.
   - ☐ If birth relatives reject me, God will stand by my side and strengthen me.

6. What is the "take away" for you from this chapter? How will your life change?

   _____

   _____

Thoughts, Insights, Goals and Prayers

_____

_____

It is only as we face our greatest adoption fears that we are able to step confidently into the role that God has chosen for us to fulfill in history. Isn't it awesome to think he planned your life in eternity past? Just think, you are about to discover your unique footprints across the sands of time! The next chapter will aid in your discovery.

PART II
THOUGHTS THAT INDICATE YOU HAVE
COME TO TERMS WITH YOUR
ADOPTION EXPERIENCE

Under His Wings
WORKBOOK

CHAPTER 10

"I have a
unique life
purpose."

The Story of Moses

Exodus 12-14

The final plague God would use to prompt Pharaoh to let His people go was the death of every firstborn son in Egypt.
Moses told the people about God's provision to protect them from this plague. Each Israelite man was to slaughter a lamb without defect and put some of its blood upon his doorpost. God then promised that when He saw the blood, He would pass over them. Thus came the name "Passover." He said, "No destructive plague will touch you when I strike Egypt" (12:13).

"That same night they are to eat the meat roasted over the fire, along with bitter herbs and bread made without yeast" (12:8).

This sacrificial act was a glimpse of the work of Jesus Christ on our behalf. He was the perfect Lamb of God, led to the slaughter at the crucifixion and whose blood continually protects and saves those who choose to appropriate this gift by faith. Just as the Israelites were commanded to eat unleavened bread for sustenance, so believers today are commanded to eat the Bread of Life, Jesus Christ, whenever they remember and celebrate his death, burial and resurrection while taking communion.

God then led the Israelites on the desert road toward the Red Sea. "By day the Lord went ahead of them in a pillar of cloud to guide them on their way and by night in a pillar of fire to give them light, so that they could travel by day or by night. Neither the pillar of cloud by day nor the pillar of fire by night left its place in front of the people" (13: 21-22).

When Pharaoh was told that the Israelites had fled, he took 600 of his best chariots, along with many other Egyptian chariots and officers. The Israelites were terrified, but Moses stepped boldly into his leadership role and said, "Do not be afraid. Stand firm and you will see the deliverance the Lord will bring you today. The Egyptians you see today you will never see again. The Lord will fight for you; you need only be still" (14: 13-14).

The Israelites continued their frantic escape, with Pharaoh on their heels. When they came to the Red Sea "…the Lord drove back the sea with a strong east wind and turned it into dry land. The waters were divided, and the Israelites went through the sea on dry ground, with a wall of water on their right and on their left" (14: 21).

All of Pharaoh's chariots and horsemen followed them into the sea and God threw confusion into their minds and made the wheels of their chariots come off. "Then the Lord said to Moses, 'Stretch out your hand over the sea so that the waters may flow back over the Egyptians and their chariots and horsemen.' Moses stretched out his hand over the sea, and at daybreak, the sea went back to its place. The Egyptians were fleeing toward it, and the Lord swept them into the sea…Not one of them survived" (14: 26-27).

When the Israelites saw the great power of the Lord, they feared God and put their trust in him and in Moses, his servant (14: 26-31).

1. How do you think Moses felt when he put his big toe in the Red Sea?

    _____

    _____

2. How do you think he felt when he saw the Red Sea part?

    _____

    _____

How Moses Saw God

Moses now saw God as **Jehovah-M'Kaddesh**, the God who sets his people apart for his peculiar possession and for his holy work. What joy Moses must have felt when he experienced the truth of II Peter 2: 9: "But you are a chosen people, a royal priesthood, a holy nation, a people belonging to God, that you may declare the praises of him who called you out of darkness and into his wonderful life."

How You See God

Please refer to the list of Names for Jesus in Scripture in Appendix B and list three to five

names for God that stand out to you. It will be encouraging to look back when finished with the

workbook and see how your perception has grown!

You can record your words here:

_____

_____

How Other Adoptees Feel

Brian Keck, between the age of 10 and 16, was placed in 27 foster homes, three adoptive placements, two group homes and one detention center. He went on to earn a degree in social work and is now dedicating himself to become an Olympic wrestler. He said in an article for *Connections*, a newsletter published by ATTACh, "The early years of my life had not been the fairytale that everybody dreams about. I feel that everybody has problems every day. The difference is how you deal with those problems. I could have felt sorry for myself and gone nowhere in life, but I decided I wanted to make something of myself. I feel like the luckiest guy in the world to be where I am now. I know that I had a bad childhood but why would I want to dwell on my past when I have a great future in front of me?"

Learning about Adoption

"Adoption isn't right or wrong, good or bad. It just IS. Whatever happened in the past can't be changed, but the decisions made about past experiences can be changed and replaced with joyful, life-supporting beliefs," write Jean Illsley Clarke and Connie Dawson in *Growing Up Again: Parenting Ourselves, Parenting Our Children.*

Putting my Feelings and Needs into Words

1. Have you ever had a "Red Sea experience?" Something that seemed impossible? Could your relinquishment be an example? How about uncovering and facing your true feelings about adoption or making a phone call to your birth mother once you have found her. Record them here.

   _____

   _____

2. What evidence is there that you have replaced painful, negative emotions with life-giving choices?

   _____

   _____

3. Is there a new boldness and confidence in your life? Please explain and give examples.

   _____

   _____

4. Look back on the last eight chapters and record how feelings and perspective are evolving.

   _____

   _____

5. What are some practical ways you could "reframe" the pain and loss from relinquishment? How can you change your outlook? Check the example statements of "reframing" with which you most agree and explain why on the lines that follow:

   ❐ Loss becomes gain, for I can now comfort friends and family that are hurting.
   ❐ Unanswered adoption questions are held in the hand of my heavenly Father.
   ❐ The hole in my heart caused by relinquishment was the very thing that made me realize my need for God.
   ❐ Rejections by friends or parents were invitations for friendship with God.
   ❐ _____

   _____

Writing Letters TO and FROM My Birth Mother and God

- Write a letter TO your birth mother and tell her how you feel about the possibility of discovering your life purpose. If you feel ready, thank her for her part in your personality.

- Write a letter FROM your birth mother, imagining how she might respond to your discovery of what she has contributed to your life.

- Write a letter TO God, asking him to show you your life purpose and spiritual gifts.

- Write a letter FROM God about he might feel as you discover spiritual gifts and life purpose.

Under His Wings
WORKBOOK

Letters TO and FROM
My Birth Mother

Digging Deep for Answers to my Adoption Questions

1. Read Esther 4:14. What did this uncle say to his adopted daughter about her life purpose?

    _____

    _____

2. Read Jeremiah 1:5. What does this verse reveal about life purpose? Can you apply it to your life?

    _____

    _____

3. Read I Corinthians 7:7. What does God state as fact in this verse?

    _____

    _____

4. Read Romans 12: 4-8 and list all the spiritual gifts.

    _____

    _____

5. Based on the gifts listed above, where do you see yourself? Where do others see you? Do they easily follow you (leadership)? Are their spirits lifted by your words (encouragement)? Do you love to teach biblical truths...can you explain them clearly (teaching)?

    _____

    _____

6. Read I Corinthians 12: 7-11. List the gifts mentioned and how these gifts are to be used.

    _____

    _____

7. How will your life change as a result of studying this chapter?

    _____

    _____

Thoughts, Insights, Goals and Prayers

_____

_____

_____

As we put our big toes into our personal Red Seas caused by the loss of our birthmothers, we begin to see God at work in every detail of life! Life becomes an exciting journey. We will talk about seeing God at work in our lives next.

Under His Wings
WORKBOOK

CHAPTER 11

"I can see how God is working in my life!"

The Story of Moses

Exodus 15

Moses had just witnessed the mighty power of God. The Red Sea parted and thousands of Israelites passed through unharmed. God confirmed to Moses that he was fulfilling his God-given role as leader through the affirmations and trust of the Israelite people. Moses was so full of praise to God for what he had done that he couldn't stop praising him. Listen to his words he sang to the Lord:

"I will sing to the Lord, for he is highly exalted. The horse and its rider he hurled into the sea.
The Lord is my strength and my song; he has become my salvation.
He is my God, and I will praise him.
The Lord is a Warrior;
The Lord is his name.
Pharaoh's chariots and his army he has hurled into the sea.
The best of Pharaoh's officers are drowned in the Red Sea.
The deep waters have covered them;
they sank to the depths like a stone.
Your right hand, O Lord, was majestic in power.
Your right hand, O Lord, shattered the enemy.
In the greatness of your majesty you threw down those who opposed you.
You unleashed your burning anger; it consumed them like stubble.
By the blast of your nostrils the waters piled up.
The surging waters stood firm like a wall; the deep waters congealed in the heart of the sea.
The enemy boasted, 'I will pursue, I will overtake them. I will divide the spoils; I will gorge myself on them. I will draw my sword and my hand will destroy them.'
They sank like lead in the mighty waters.
Who among the gods is like you, O Lord?
Who is like you—majestic in holiness, awesome in glory, working wonders?
You stretched out your right hand and the earth swallowed them.
In your unfailing love you will lead the people you have redeemed.
In your strength you will guide them to your holy dwelling.
The nations will hear and tremble; anguish will grip the people of Philista.
The chiefs of Edom will be terrified, the leaders of Moab will be seized with trembling, the people of Canaan will melt away; terror and dread will fall upon them.
By the power of your arm they will be as still as a stone—until your people pass by.
You will bring them in and plant them on the mountain of your inheritance—the place, O Lord, your hands have established. The Lord will reign forever and ever" (15: 1-18).

1. Look back over the song of Moses and circle all the words that describe God.

2. Which is the most meaningful to you and why?

3. Draw a picture of Moses as he sings his song to the Lord.

4. If you had been in Moses' presence while he sang his song, what would you say in response to him? ("That was pretty weird." "Wow, you make me want to know God more!" "What a beautiful, powerful expression of your love for God!" "You sure are religious, Moses.")

_____

_____

How Moses Saw God

Moses had come to know God as **Jehovah-shalom,** the God of all peace. This is the deepest need of the human heart—to be at peace with God and with oneself. The proof that his heart was at peace was that it was filled with praise...not necessarily for what God had done, but for who God is. He was living out the chief end of man—to glorify God and enjoy him forever. Psalm 29:11 says, "The Lord gives strength to his people; the Lord blesses his people with peace."

How You See God

Please refer to the list of Names for Jesus in Scripture in Appendix B and list three to five

names for God that stand out to you. It will be encouraging to look back when finished with the

workbook and see how your perception has grown!

You can record your words here:

_____

_____

How Other Adoptees Feel

Dr. Richard B. Gilbert, in an article entitled "Bereavement Challenges and Pathways for the Adopted" appearing in *Jewel Among Jewels Adoption News*, writes, "Through faith searching, a wonderful wife and family, supportive friends, and a new stubborn determination to be 'free,' I have recognized my right and need to affirm my God-given goodness...I have learned to see adoption not as a mark or scar, but as a gift."

Sherrie Eldridge writes, "When I was a brand new Christian, my husband and I, along with our two young daughters, were taking a trip across country to visit relatives. As a new believer, I was silently praising God (my husband was not a Christian) as we drove through the Rocky Mountains. "What a beautiful creation God made for us to enjoy," I silently said to myself. "Even the pine trees reach up to him!" At one point, the scenery was particularly spectacular. So spectacular that we got out of the car at a lookout point to take photos. When it was time to go, we realized we had a problem-- we had locked the keys inside the car. Not a soul was insight, nor was there a gas station for miles. My husband panicked. I prayed. A few minutes later, a handsome young man in a beat-up jeep stopped to see what was the matter. When we told him that we had locked our keys in the car, he said, "Oh, don't worry about that," he jokingly said. "I'm an old Chicago car thief!" With that, he returned to his Jeep, brought a wire coat hanger and proceeded to bend it carefully into a shape that could be inserted through the rim of the window. In seconds, the door was unlocked!

We thanked him profusely as he drove off. I know that his arrival on the scene was no coincidence. God sent him to help us. I wondered at the time if he could have been an angel in disguise. My husband took note of the miraculous intervention and began to see a loving God who is involved in the lives of his children. Each one of us felt his presence as he made himself so real to us that day."

Check the statements with which you most agree and explain why on the lines that follow:

- ☐ Now I am glad that I was adopted!
- ☐ I don't know what my life would have been like had I not been adopted.
- ☐ I can see now why I was removed from the care of my birth family.
- ☐ I need to be reminded that God redeems the pain of adoption and works it for my good and his glory.

_____

_____

_____

_____

_____

_____

_____

Appreciating Life
-Sherrie Eldridge

As children of God, we are all in the wonderful process of being healed by the Great Physician, Jesus. His healing can be evidenced in newfound appreciation, as we learn to enjoy him and the life he has given us.

Webster's defines "appreciation" as, "To be grateful for; to value highly; to place a high estimate on; to be fully aware of; to prize; to exercise wise judgment; delicate perception and keen insight into the worth of something."

As I took time to look back over the last few years and identify the most hurtful experiences, there came a new desire to praise God for the trials. See if you identify with any of these statements, check the ones with which you most agree:

- ❏ I didn't appreciate the acceptance of Christ until I had been utterly rejected.
- ❏ I didn't appreciate his strength until I allowed myself to become weak.
- ❏ I didn't appreciate his loyalty until another betrayed me.
- ❏ I didn't appreciate his grace until I fell flat on my face.
- ❏ I didn't appreciate family living close by until they moved far away.
- ❏ I didn't appreciate the Lord's trust in me until I knew the sting of persecution.
- ❏ I didn't appreciate the light of the Lord's countenance until I sat in darkness.
- ❏ I didn't appreciate the healing balm of Gilead until I had been deeply wounded.
- ❏ I didn't appreciate the comforting shoulder of a friend until my heart had been broken.
- ❏ I didn't appreciate the abiding presence of the Holy Spirit until I felt totally abandoned.
- ❏ I didn't appreciate intimacy with God until I spent time in the desert.
- ❏ I didn't appreciate the hope of heaven until I buried a loved one.
- ❏ I didn't appreciate Jesus as Lord until my life became unmanageable.
- ❏ I didn't appreciate Jesus as my Life until I came to the absolute end of my own resources.

Learning about Adoption
Adoption specialist, James Gritter, writes in his book *The Spirit of Open Adoption*, "At heart, adoption is truly a spiritual relationship..."

Putting My Feelings and Needs into Words

1. When and where has your heart been filled with praise because you knew that God was working in your behalf through the circumstances?

_____

_____

2. What can you praise God for in regard to your adoption? For example, a birth mother who gave you the gift of birth, adoptive parents who gave you a home and loving family when you had none, etc.

_____

_____

3. Why is adoption a spiritual experience?

_____

_____

4. What do you think are the differences between human and spiritual adoption?

_____

_____

5. Is everyone an adopted child of God? See John 3: 5-7.

_____

_____

6. Have you been spiritually adopted? Spiritual adoption means that you realize that in God's eyes, you are a sinner. You have failed to love him every moment of every day. He has already forgiven you of your sins—past, present, and future. But this wonderful gift doesn't become yours until you agree with him that you are a sinner in need of salvation, ask him to cleanse you and then fill you with his blessed Holy Spirit. Why not find a quiet place to kneel down and do just that?

_____

_____

7. God will confirm to you that you have been spiritually adopted in several ways:
   • The Bible will come alive to you and you will find it applies to your life.
   • You will want to read your Bible and pray.
   • You will want to be with other Christians.
   • Others will see that you have changed.
   • You will want to join a local church.
   • You will want to share with others what God is doing in your life.
   • God will make himself real to you.
   • You will be assured that you belong to Jesus through the indwelling Holy Spirit.

Writing Letters TO and FROM My Birth Mother and God

• Write a letter TO your birth mother, thanking her, if you feel so inclined, for carrying you for nine months and choosing to give you the gift of birth.

• Write a letter FROM your birth mother, telling you how she feels about God at work in your life.

• It is impossible to praise God for your adoption until you have forgiven your birth parents for placing you for adoption. Forgiveness is a choice. An act of the will. Write a letter TO God, telling Him how you feel about forgiving.

• Write a letter FROM God to you about forgiveness.

Under His Wings
WORKBOOK

Letters TO and FROM
My Birth Mother

_____

_____

_____

_____

_____

_____

_____

_____

_____

_____

_____

_____

_____

_____

_____

_____

_____

_____

_____

_____

_____

Under His Wings
WORKBOOK

Letters TO and FROM
God

_____

_____

_____

_____

_____

_____

_____

_____

_____

_____

_____

_____

_____

_____

_____

_____

_____

_____

Digging Deep for Answers to my Adoption Questions

1. God told Moses that he would give a sign to him that he had successfully brought the Israelites out of bondage. The sign was "…you will worship God on this mountain" (Exodus 3: 12b). Are you able to worship God as Moses did in his song? Or is your heart still crippled by an unforgiving spirit toward God for touching your life with adoption, or your birth mother for relinquishing you?

    _____

    _____

2. David Augsburger, in *Caring Enough to Forgive/Caring Enough Not to Forgive* lists these requirements for forgiveness:
    * Let it be. Say goodbye to predicaments, problems, and failures.
    * Let go of demands, defenses and disgust.
    * Say goodbye to the past. Be present in this moment.
    * Risk. Reach out to the future with trust.

    Where are you in this process? If you haven't said goodbye to the pain of the past and embraced forgiveness, what is needed?

    _____

    _____

3. What does the apostle Paul say should happen after forgiveness? See Philippians 3: 13.

    _____

    _____

4. How will your life change as a result of studying this chapter?

    _____

    _____

Thoughts, Insights, Goals and Prayers

_____

_____

It is no easy task to forgive, but God commands us to, for his glory and our good. Unforgiveness hurts no one but us. However, when we *do* choose to forgive, the circumstances and people that trigger feelings of rejection begin to lose their power over us.

Under His Wings
WORKBOOK

CHAPTER 12

"I can now
take rejection
in stride."

The Story of Moses

Exodus 15

An incredible victory had just occurred! The sea had parted, the Israelites had gone through on dry land and Pharaoh's army had been hurled into the sea. What celebrating must have occurred in the camp! Miriam could hardly contain herself. She picked up her tambourine and joyously began leading the women in song and dance. The crowd went wild!

You would think such victory would be accompanied by a continuous and overwhelming gratefulness to God for his guidance through Moses, but that wasn't the case. There was gratefulness, but only for a few days. Gratefulness transformed into grumbling when Moses led them into the Desert of Shur where there was no good drinking water. "For three days they traveled in the desert without finding water. When they came to Marah, they could not drink its water because it was bitter" (v. 22-24).

As a seasoned leader, Moses knew that blessing always follows battle. Thus, he prayed, threw a piece of wood into the bitter waters as God commanded and then watched, as the water became miraculously sweet.

The Lord told the people that the bitter water episode was a test. A test in which they failed to trust and obey him. "If you will begin listening carefully to my voice and do what is right in my sight, I won't bring any of the Egyptian plagues on you, for I am the Lord who heals you" (v. 26).
Following close on the heels of the miraculous provision of sweet water was a second test—this time in another desert, the Desert of Sin. What an appropriate name, for the people committed the same sin—they grumbled against Moses. "If only we could die. Why are you leading us in such a round-about way to the Promised Land? Egypt was better. At least we had all the food we wanted. But here we are literally starving to death," they probably said.

Moses rebuked the people, saying that their grumbling was not against him, but against the Lord. What a giant step in growth for this adoptee! He didn't take the rejection personally! What boldness and what a contrast to the Moses who once had said, "I don't have anything to say." Moses had changed from a people pleaser into a God pleaser.

Meanwhile, the gracious God, instead of giving the grumblers what they deserved, gave instead another miracle. It happened one morning when they came out of their tents and noticed a dewy-like substance on the ground. Moses explained that it was manna—bread from heaven, which was to be gathered each day according to each person's need. "I will see whether they follow my instructions to gather only enough for one day," God may have said. "This will be their test."
The people failed the test again. They didn't obey God's command to only gather manna for six days and keep the Sabbath day holy.

In spite of God's goodness in the years that followed, the people continued grumbling, even going so far as to question whether the Lord was really among them. In the midst of the grumbling, their enemies, the Amalekites, attacked. Moses backed off from active leadership at this juncture and gave his "son in the faith," Joshua, an opportunity to grow. Joshua would take the troops into battle while Moses prayed for them.

Thus, with the staff of God in hand, Moses ascended the hill to pray. As long as he held up his staff, the Israelites won. However, as the battle raged on, Moses grew weary and asked Aaron and Hur to hold up his hands. This was another triumph for Moses! He threw off his former I-can-handle-anything exterior and asked for help from others.

When the battle was won, Moses built an altar and called it "The Lord is my Banner."

1. What inner struggles do you think Moses experienced when the people grumbled and rejected his leadership?

    _____

    _____

2. Why didn't the rejection disturb him?

    _____

    _____

How Moses Saw God

Moses perceived God as **Jehovah-nissi**; "The Lord Is My Banner." A banner was a standard of victory carried at the head of a military band to indicate the line of march, or rallying point. God was the rallying point for Moses and the troops. Exodus 17:15 records his words: "The Lord is my banner…For hands were lifted up to the throne of the Lord. The Lord will be at war against the Amalekites from generation to generation."

How You See God

Please refer to the list of Names for Jesus in Scripture in Appendix B and list three to five names for God that stand out to you. It will be encouraging to look back when finished with the workbook and see how your perception has grown!

    You can record your words here:

_____

_____

How Other Adoptees Feel

See if you identify with any of these statements, check the ones with which you most agree:
- ❏ I am tired of trying to please people.
- ❏ I sometimes feel like I can't throw off my "I-can-handle-anything" exterior and ask for help from others.
- ❏ I need to learn to ask for and receive help from others.
- ❏ When I go to the Lord in prayer, my battles don't seem so bad.
- ❏ Lately I am surprised by my resilience when others reject me.
- ❏ I don't "read" rejection into every situation like I used to.

A Banner Like None Other
--Sherrie Eldridge

"He brought me to the banqueting house, and his banner over me was love" (Song of Solomon 2: 4).

Suppose for a moment that you are a university coed on your way to a Saturday afternoon football game with your sweetheart. (This might be difficult for male readers, but do the best you can)!

Autumn leaves paint a glorious palette of color around the path toward the stadium and the sound of the gathering crowd fills the air. The smell of fresh caramel corn wafts through the air and vendors sell mums with pipe-cleaner letters.

As you enter the stadium, your sweetheart takes your hand and leads you to your seats for a great afternoon of entertainment.

"Life doesn't get much better than this," you say to yourself.

As the marching band lines up for the pre-game show, small planes with advertising banners buzz overhead. One particular banner catches your attention immediately, for it spells out a familiar word— your first name!

After your name are three simple words: I LOVE YOU!

"Somebody really wanted to get their message across," you figure. When you glance at your sweetheart to see if he saw the same plane, you notice a twinkle in his eyes and a smile on his face.

"Do you know something about that banner that I don't know?" you ask.

When the band conductor signals the crowd to stand for the fight song, everyone rises, except the two of you. As the crowd sings, your sweetheart pulls you close and pulls out a small gift box.

"Go ahead! Open it up," he says.

Your eyes well with tears and your heart thumps. Inside the gift box is another box, hinged and covered with silk. Again, he invites you to open it up. As you do, you discover a golden engagement ring, which he removes from the box and places on your finger.

"Honey, will you marry me?" he says. "I want to spend the rest of my life with you."

What a story! "That only happens in fairy tales," you may be muttering under your breath.
Let me share how that fairy tale comes alive day after day in the lives of those who love and follow Jesus.

How like the sweetheart is Jesus, the Lover of our souls, who courts us daily. How like the couple on the stadium bench, oblivious to everyone around them are you and I as we enjoy intimacy with Jesus in the midst of this crazy world. How like the sweetheart who went to extraordinary lengths to demonstrate his love by having his message of love unfurling behind a plane, did the heavenly Father in sending his only Son to die for us at Calvary. How like the words of proposal spoken to the coed are the words of Jesus…"I want to spend eternity with you."

The analogies are endless. But perhaps in the midst of our hectic days, we should take a look at his banner flying over us. And as we do, we will delight in its message once again: (Put your name here)...I LOVE YOU!

Learning about Adoption

Perhaps one of the greatest battles for an adoptee is giving up people pleasing and not taking rejection personally. Ronald Nydam, Ph.D., in an article entitled "Doing Rejection" appearing in *Jewel Among Jewels Adoption News* said, "The task of all adoptees is to finally relinquish their relinquishment; that is, to really accept the decision of the birth parents to carry out their plan for adoption. If the original relinquishment is not relinquished, the adoptee may chronically hang on to the primal connection in such a way that she is never free to be fully adult. Doing rejection successfully means opening the door to a full life as an adult who can do self-acceptance and intimacy in spite of a birth parent's negative opinion."

Putting my Feelings and Needs into Words

1. Are you driven to please others? If so, what are some of the ways you have tried to win the love and acceptance of others?

   _____

   _____

2. What is the most painful opposition or rejection you have experienced?

   _____

   _____

3. When you are faced with rejection, what are your options and needs?

   _____

   _____

4. Have you "relinquished your relinquishment?" How? When?

   _____

   _____

A Drawing for My Birth Mother

Draw a picture of yourself atop a mountain, plunging a banner of victory into the ground. Why not make this the day that you relinquish your relinquishment and see the Lord as your banner?

Draw a picture of yourself and your birth mother after you relinquish your relinquishment.

1. "He has taken me to the banquet hall, and his banner over me is love" (Song of Solomon 2: 4). Meditate on this verse and then ask yourself:

    • What would the banquet hall look like?

    • What would Jesus look like? (Just think…he is the one who will meet ALL your needs).

    • What would he say to you?

    • What would you say to him?

    • What color is the banner?

    • What does the banner say? (What words does he use to convey his personal love?)

2. Read Isaiah 54:17. If you think about rejection as a weapon that is formed by Satan to destroy you, what does God promise and what does that mean to you?

    _____

    _____

3. Joseph of the Bible was rejected by his brothers and sold into slavery in Egypt. Joseph walked so closely with God that he found favor in the eyes of the Pharaoh and was put in a high position of authority. When a famine came in the land where his rejecting brothers lived, they came to him, asking for food. Joseph's response in Genesis 50: 20 says a lot about how he viewed rejection. What did he say to his brothers? How can you apply this to your life?

    _____

    _____

4. What is the "take away" for you from this chapter?

    _____

    _____

Thoughts, Insights, Goals and Prayers

Rejection can roll off you like water off a duck's back! Like Joseph, you will be able to trust in the fact that any rejection life can throw at you will always be turned for your good if you belong to God. The need for approval from people will be replaced with a deep desire to have an intimate relationship with God. We are then able to come full circle with our adoption experience and learn to see it through God's eyes. We begin to see that indeed, we were adopted for a purpose. This will be our topic for the last chapter.

Under His Wings
WORKBOOK

CHAPTER 13

"I am amazed
that God
wants to be
my friend."

The Story of Moses

Exodus 19-33

Moses didn't know it, but he was about to enter an intimate relationship with God.

The Lord said to Moses, "I am going to come to you in a dense cloud, so that the people will hear me speaking with you and will always put their trust in you" (Exodus 19: 9).

"For six days the cloud covered the mountain, and on the seventh day the Lord called to Moses from within the cloud. To the Israelites the glory of the Lord looked like a consuming fire on top of the mountain. Then Moses entered the cloud as he went on up the mountain. And he stayed on the mountain 40 days and 40 nights" (Exodus 24: 16).

It was there that Moses received the Ten Commandments and other laws that the Israelites were to obey as they entered the Promised Land. When Moses returned to the people and relayed God's words, they said, "Everything the Lord has said we will do" (Exodus 24: 3).

Moses then returned to the top of the mountain to have fellowship with God. It was there that he was given another assignment—to build a temporary dwelling place where God could commune with man. The tent, as it was called, was just one cog in the wheel of communion with man, one movement in the opening of the beautiful flower of fellowship. It was here that God became a pilgrim with the pilgrims.

How this delighted the heart of God, for ever since the Garden of Eden, when Adam sinned and brought separation from God for himself and the entire human race, God yearned for fellowship with man. "Let them make me a sanctuary that I may dwell among them" (Exodus 25:8). Up on the mountain with God, Moses was given specific instructions for setting up the tabernacle. God said, "Set up the tabernacle according to the plan shown you on the mountain" (Exodus 26: 30).

This was to be a temporary meeting place, for it only lasted 400 years. Following that, the temple was made. Years later, the body of Jesus Christ became the temple—that is why he is called "Emmanuel," meaning "God with us" (Matthew 1: 23). In our day, God's temple is the heart of every believer in Jesus Christ through the indwelling Holy Spirit. "Don't you know that you yourselves are God's temple and that God's Spirit lives in you" (I Corinthians 3:16)?

Whenever the people saw the pillar of cloud standing at the entrance of the tent, they all stood and worshipped. "The Lord would speak to Moses face-to-face, as a man speaks to his friend" (Exodus 33:11). What a privilege for this adoptee—friendship with God! God offers this friendship today to *all* who will come to him by faith.

God then tenderly ministered to Moses' vulnerable spot—the fear of abandonment. He said, "My presence will go with you, and I will give you rest" (Exodus 33:14).

1. What is your most vulnerable spot when it comes to adoption?

   _____

   _____

2. What do you think it would be like to have friendship with God?

How Moses Saw God

Moses was getting to know God as **Emmanuel**, which means "God with us." "The virgin will be with child and will give birth to a son, and they will call him 'Emmanuel'—which means 'God with us'" (Matthew 1: 23).

How You See God

Please refer to the list of Names for Jesus in Scripture in Appendix B and list three to five names for God that stand out to you. It will be encouraging to look back when finished with the workbook and see how your perception has grown!

You can record your words here:

_____

_____

How Other Adoptees Feel

Check the statements with which you agree and explain why you checked them on the lines that follow:
- ❏ I need to be intimately united with someone who will never leave me. Friends and family all leave eventually through death, but there is one that will take me through death and home to heaven.
- ❏ I have always had difficulty with intimacy. I get scared when others get too close to the real me.
- ❏ I need the indwelling Holy Spirit, who will remind me that God will never abandon me.
- ❏ Is it *really* possible to be a friend of God?
- ❏ I need a best friend. I have not been able to get close to people in the past, let alone God.

_____

_____

_____

_____

_____

Learning about Adoption

Thomas Patrick Malone, M.D., and Patrick Thomas Malone, M.D., in their book, *The Art of Intimacy*, say, "*Intimacy* is derived from the Latin *intima*, meaning 'inner' or 'innermost.' Your inside being is the real you, the you that only you can know. The problem is that you can know it only when you are being intimate with something or someone outside yourself. Intimate itself is a revealing word. As an adjective it means 'personal,' 'private,' 'detailed,' 'deep,' 'innermost.' As a noun it describes a close friend or associate. As a verb it means 'to make known indirectly' or 'to hint at.' This sense of touching our innermost core is the essence of intimacy."

Putting my Feelings and Needs into Words

1. What do you believe are the basic components of friendship?

   _____

   _____

2. How does it make you feel to know that God wants to be your best friend?

   _____

   _____

3. Can you identify any roadblocks that are hindering a friendship with God? If so, what are they?

   _____

   _____

Writing Letters TO and FROM My Birth Mother, My Adoptive Mother, and God

- Write a letter TO your birth mother about where you are in your journey and how you feel about it.
- Write a letter FROM your birth mother expressing how you believe she might feel when learning about your growth.
- Write a letter TO your adoptive parents, telling them how you feel about them at this point in time.
- Write a letter FROM your adoptive parents. How are they doing in this process of your healing? Imagine how your deepening relationship with God would affect them and write your letter accordingly.
- Write a letter TO God about the possibility of having friendship with him.
- Write a letter FROM God to you.

Letters TO and FROM
My Birth Mother

_____

_____

_____

_____

_____

_____

_____

_____

_____

_____

_____

_____

_____

_____

_____

_____

_____

_____

_____

_____

_____

Under His Wings
WORKBOOK

Under His Wings
WORKBOOK

Digging Deep for Answers to my Adoption Questions

1. Read Proverbs 17:17. What are two attributes of a friend?

   _____

   _____

2. Read Proverbs 18:24b. Who is this referring to?

   _____

   _____

3. What does Jesus promise to his friends in John 15:15?

   _____

   _____

4. What changes will occur in your life this week after reading and applying this chapter?

   _____

   _____

Thoughts, Insights, Goals and Prayers

_____

_____

Now that friendship with God has begun, your focus is changing. You are receiving so much love and support from God that you want to reach out to others and help them grow. We will talk about that next.

CHAPTER 14

"I enjoy helping others grow!"

The Story of Moses

Numbers 12-14

Moses knew it was time to pass on the baton of leadership to Hoshea, the young man he had been grooming since childhood. He had been like a father to Hoshea. Nurturing him. Instructing him. Teaching him the ways of God. Hoshea's initiation into leadership occurred when Moses asked him to lead the army in battle against the Amalekites, which we talked about earlier. And lead the army he did! He and the choice men accompanying him overcame the Amalekites with the sword.

Later, Moses invited Hoshea to be his aide when he went to meet God on the mountain and ratify the covenant between God and man. What a thrill it must have been for Hoshea to accompany Moses up the mountain and how rewarding it must have been for Moses to see this young man growing in strength and stature.

Years later Moses commanded Hoshea and his friend Caleb to lead a band of men to explore Canaan, the Promised Land. It was a turning point in the mentoring of Hoshea because Moses changed his name from Hoshea to Joshua, which means, "the Lord is salvation."

Joshua's faith and courage surfaced during this trip, for all the other men except his friend Caleb, were terrified of the people inhabiting the land.
Joshua and Caleb returned with a positive report: "The land we passed through and explored is exceedingly good. If the Lord is pleased with us, he will lead us into that land, a land flowing with milk and honey, and will give it to us" (Numbers 14: 6-8)

God was disgusted with the people's rebellion and the unbelief of the other men that accompanied Joshua. As a result, he only allowed Caleb and Joshua to enter the Promised Land. The rest would wander and die in the wilderness.

The Lord then gave Moses some crushing news—he wouldn't be able to enter the Promised Land. He would only see it from a distance.

"You shall not enter it, either. But your assistant Joshua, son of Nun, will enter it. Encourage him, because he will lead Israel to inherit it"(Deuteronomy 1: 38).

Moses harbored no bitterness. Once he knew God's will, he took the necessary steps to put Joshua into service. At this turning point, he penned another song, choosing to praise God in all situations-- even situations he didn't understand. No wonder God called Moses the most humble man on earth. "Now Moses was a very humble man, more humble than anyone else on earth" (Numbers 12:3).

1. How do you think Moses felt as he saw Joshua live out all that he had taught him in his youth?

   _____

   _____

2. Sometimes adoptees find it hard to let go of mentoring relationships. Is this ever true of you? If so, when?

   _____

   _____

How Moses Saw God

The words of his song recorded in Deuteronomy 32 reveal his concept of God: "Oh, praise the greatness of the Lord"; "Rock"; "Father who makes and forms you"; "like an eagle that stirs up its nest and hovers over its young, that spreads its wings to catch them and carries them on its pinions"; "the God who gave you birth." It is obvious that Moses knew God as **Adonai,** the Sovereign Lord, Master of our lives and service. He alone is the head over all.

How You See God

Please refer to the list of Names for Jesus in Scripture in Appendix B and list three to five names for God that stand out to you. It will be encouraging to look back when finished with the workbook and see how your perception has grown!

You can record your words here:

_____

_____

How Other Adoptees Feel

Check the statements with which you agree and explain why you checked them on the lines that follow:
- ❏ I am in awe to think that God would use me to help shape the life of one of his future leaders.
- ❏ I need a mentor. Someone who is further along on their journey than me.
- ❏ I find it very difficult when there is a change in leadership. Change is very difficult for me. I had already bonded with one leader and then he left.
- ❏ I need encouragement from a godly person.
- ❏ You are like the mother I never had or never will have.
- ❏ You are a safe haven to me.
- ❏ Can you see me here cheering you on?
- ❏ It is a privilege for me to "mother" your precious soul.
- ❏ I believe in you!
- ❏ You are a spiritual mother/father to me.

_____

_____

A Letter from Sherrie Eldridge's Writing Mentor
-Traci Mullins

My dear baby duck, I think back so many years ago to a tiny duck named Sherrie who approached me with an idea for a book about her painful experience of reuniting with her birth mother. I knew she needed to write, write, write…for her own sake. For a catharsis. For her healing. She needed a little more time in the "nest" where she could be safe before heading out into the big wide world where everyone would know her story. She needed to mine for the jewels deep within her own soul before she could begin handing them out as gifts to others. And now…she has transformed from a tiny duck into a lovely swan, beautiful and confident and strong enough to help other tiny ducks learn to fly. She has metamorphosed from a fledgling writer with journal and pen to a brilliant, real author who's even mastering the computer! Most of all, she has become a whole woman God is using in profound ways…which have only just begun. I am so proud of her.

I love you, dear Sherrie! Mama Duck

Learning About Adoption

The selections for this section may be difficult to understand. The first piece is written for mental health clinicians and the second for seasoned Bible students. In spite of this, scan the paragraphs and mark the words or phrases that apply to you.

Malcolm I. West and Adrienne E. Sheldon-Keller, in *Patterns of Relating: An Adult Attachment Perspective*, write, "The securely attached adult can acknowledge felt distress...and turn to supportive and trusted relationships for comfort. Particularly during periods of emotional upset, comfort often needs to be expressed in concrete attachment behaviors that reassure the individual. Put simply, felt security at these times has a lot to do with having someone available who will respond to our feelings and even take supportive action. The special warmth that often accompanies attachment comes just from these tangible reassurances that one is understood."

Oswald Chambers, in his devotional book, *My Utmost for His Highest*, describes the mentoring relationship between Elijah (the mentor) and Elisha. It would be helpful to read the account in II Kings 2.

THIS EXPERIENCE MUST COME
"And he saw him no more." II Kings ii.12.
It is not wrong to depend upon Elijah as long as God gives him to you, but remember the time will come when he will have to go; when he stands no more to you as your guide and leader, because God does not intend that he should. You say, "I cannot go on without Elijah." God says you must.
Alone at your Jordan. v.14. Jordan is the type of separation where there is no fellowship with anyone else, and where no one can take the responsibility for you. You have to put to the test now what you learned when you were with your Elijah. You have been to Jordan over and over again with Elijah, but now you are up against it alone. It is no use in saying you cannot go. If you want to know whether God is God you have faith to believe him to be, then go through your Jordan alone.
Alone at your Jericho. v. 15. Jericho is the place where you have seen your Elijah do great things. When you come to your Jericho you have a strong disinclination to take the initiative and trust in God, you want someone else to take it for you. If you remain true to what you learned with your Elijah, you will get the sign that God is with you.
Alone at Bethel. v. 23. At your Bethel you will find yourself at your wits' end and at the beginning of God's wisdom. When you get to your wits' end and feel inclined to succumb to panic, don't. Stand true to God and he will bring his truth out in a way that will make your life a sacrament. Put into practice what you learned with your Elijah, use his cloak and pray. Determine to trust in God and do not look for Elijah any more.

Putting My Feelings and Needs into Words

1. Are you at the point in your journey where, like Moses, you can lift someone else up on your shoulders so that he/she can be successful? If so, who?

_____

_____

2. What are your emotional and spiritual needs as you mentor others? And what are some healthy ways of getting those needs met?

_____

_____

3. What do you believe is the greatest gift a mentor can give?

    _____

    _____

4. Have you ever had a mentor? If so, who? What did they do to encourage you?

    _____

    _____

5. If you haven't had a mentor, whom would you choose? Why?

    _____

    _____

6. If you have mentored others, describe your method of encouraging.

    _____

    _____

Draw a simple line drawing on the following page, using stick figures to represent each mentor. Show how they humbled themselves in order to lift you up on their shoulders so that you could thrive and grow. Your first mentor should be on the bottom, the next on his/her shoulders, etc. If you have had no mentors, make a line drawing of yourself, expressing your desire for one, if you feel this way.

Digging Deep for Answers to My Adoption Questions

1. Record Psalm 91:4. This verse bears repeating. Where is the safest place to be when you are afraid to go on without your mentor? Or when you are overwhelmed with adoption issues?

   _____

   _____

2. In I Thessalonians 1:7, Paul describes his behavior as a mentor. What were the characteristics of his mentoring?

   _____

   _____

3. If "gentleness" is the prominent characteristic of a mentor, what would you look for in seeking a mentor, based on Webster's definition of gentleness? Check the bulleted points that apply:

- ❏ Kind
- ❏ Tender
- ❏ Gracious
- ❏ Thoughtful
- ❏ Merciful
- ❏ Compassionate
- ❏ Considerate
- ❏ Sweet-tempered
- ❏ Calm
- ❏ Gentle-hearted
- ❏ Absence of bad temper
- ❏ Forbearance in dealing with others
- ❏ Soothing

4. Have you demonstrated the quality of gentleness to those who look up to you? Which words from the above definition are true of you and which ones do you need God's help?

_____

_____

5. Read Numbers 11:12. What words from this verse describe Moses' behavior and attitude toward his followers?

_____

_____

6. If you don't have a mentor, someone who can love you unconditionally and encourage you, it may be that you need to seek one out. Read John 16: 24 and record God's promise to you as you seek a mentor.

_____

_____

7. What is the "take away" from this chapter? How will your life be different?

_____

_____

Thoughts, Insights, Goals and Prayers

_____

_____

_____

_____

Under His Wings
WORKBOOK

CHAPTER 15

"I can now see my adoption through God's eyes!"

The Story of Moses

Numbers 11, 27

Deuteronomy 33-34

The time of Moses' death was fast approaching. He was at the ripe old age of 120.

"Then the Lord said to Moses, 'Go up to this mountain of Abarim, and see the land which I have given the sons of Israel. When you have seen it, you too will be gathered to your people" (Numbers 27: 12-13).

Moses must have wept as he stood with the people on the banks of the Jordan River, looking across to the Promised Land. How dear they had become to him! He had carried them "as a nurse carries a nursing infant" right up to the border of the land which they had spent a lifetime searching for (Numbers 11:12). Standing together on the riverbank, he gave his final blessing. Adoption themes are woven throughout. One sentence in particular revealed his perception of adoption. "The eternal God is your refuge, and underneath are the everlasting arms" (Deuteronomy 33: 27).

As he said these words, it was as if his life passed before him. Looking all the way back to his birth, he saw the arms of Jochebed, his birth mother, holding and nursing him. He saw the arms of his adoptive mother, Hatshepsut, rescuing him from death, caring for him and loving him. But beneath all those arms, he saw another set of arms holding him securely—the everlasting arms of God.
Even though his heart was breaking, he took every opportunity to minister to the needs of God's people.

First he reminded them of their position with God. He said, "Let the beloved of the Lord rest secure in him, for he shields him all day long, and the one the Lord loves rests between his shoulders" (Deuteronomy 33:12).

Secondly, he reiterated God's opinion of them. "For you are a people holy to the Lord your God. The Lord your God has chosen you out of all the peoples on the face of the earth to be his people, his treasured possession. The Lord did not set his affection on you and choose you because you were more numerous than other peoples, for you were the fewest of all peoples. But it was because the Lord loved you and kept the oath he swore to your forefathers that he brought you out with a mighty hand and redeemed you from the land of slavery, from the power of Pharaoh, king of Egypt. Know therefore that the Lord your God is God; he is the faithful God, keeping His covenant of love to a thousand generations of those who love him and keep his commands" (Deuteronomy 7: 6-9).

Afterwards, he climbed to the highest part of the mountain where he could see a spectacular view of the Promised Land. The faithfulness and goodness of God were the last things he saw before he took his last breath.

Afterwards, the same arms that carried him throughout life became the arms that carried his body to the grave. God was taking such intimate care of his own, for "no man knows his burial place to this day" (Deuteronomy 34: 6)
.

Moses, the adoptee, had been the object of God's special care from birth until death. He had now received the ultimate healing—death. He was finally at home, face to face with the Lord he adored.

1. Do you think Moses was afraid of death? Why or why not?

   _____

   _____

2. Read John 8: 51. What will each Christian see at the time of death?

   _____

   _____

How Moses Saw God

Moses now was coming to the end of his walk with God here on earth and he saw Him as **Abba**, which means "father." He realized that his heavenly Father had carried him from the womb to the tomb.

Take a close look at how Moses' concept of God enlarged and changed during his life time:
- **Jehovah**, the Being who is absolutely Self-Existent, the One who in himself possesses essential life and permanent existence.
- **El-Shaddai**, the Mighty One and Source of satisfaction
- **Jehoval-rophe**, the Healer of life's sicknesses and sorrows
- **Jehovah-shammah**, the God who makes his presence real
- **Jehovah-jireh**, the One who will provide the sacrificial lamb (Jesus) for my redemption
- **El Roi**, the God who sees
- **Jehovah-tsidkenu,** the God of righteousness and the only one who gives acceptance
- **Jehovah-rohi**, the Shepherd
- **Jehovah-M Kaddesh**, the God who sets me apart for his peculiar possession and to his holy service
- **Jehovah-shalom,** the God of all peace
- **Jehovah-nissi**, the God who is my Standard of victory in life's conflicts
- **Emmanuel**, God with us
- **Adonai**, the Sovereign Lord and Master of my life and service
- **Abba**, my Heavenly Father

Now look back over the last 12 chapters and chart how your concept of God has changed. It is not necessary to use the Hebrew terms. Just put it in your own words.

_____

_____

_____

_____

_____

How Other Adoptees Feel

Check the statements with which you agree and explain why you checked them on the lines that follow:

☐ It's awesome to know that God's arms were the arms supporting my birth and adoptive mothers' arms.

☐ I need to know that when I die, I will not see death, but only the face of Jesus Christ, my Lord and Savior.

☐ I feel overwhelmed as I look back at God's care for me throughout my life.

☐ It's really true! God does keep his promise to never leave me or forsake me.

☐ I don't feel alone anymore.

☐ I now know I was adopted for a purpose—his purpose.

_____

_____

_____

Learning about Adoption

The Missing Face
-Sherrie Eldridge
An adoptee searches for a face in a crowd that resembles her own, believing that if she could only see the face of her lost birth mother, the hurt would magically disappear. The grief would be resolved. The life-long repercussions of losing our birth mother would evaporate.

Though we may search, reunite and even rejoice together with our birth relatives, there is still another missing face. It is the face of the one in whose image we were created. The face of the one who loved us so much that he died for us. The face of Jesus Christ. The moment we see him face to face in heaven, every need will be satisfied and every tear wiped away. The healing will be complete and the validation unimaginable.

Perhaps David was referring to this when he penned the words of Psalm 17:15: 'And I—in righteousness I will see your face; when I awake, I will be satisfied with seeing your likeness."
A single thread in a tapestry
Though its color brightly shine
Can never see its purpose
In the pattern of the grand design.
And the stone that sits on the very top
Of the mountain's mighty face,
Does it think it's more important
Than the stones that form the base?
So how can you see what your life is worth?
Or where your value lies?
You can never see through the eyes of man.
You must look at your life,
Look at your life through heaven's eyes.♦
(Printed with permission from *Destiny and Deliverance: Spiritual Insights from the Life of Moses*)

The Awesome Legacy of the Orphan
-Sherrie Eldridge

Perhaps when all is said and done, beneath the anger of many adoptees is the primal fear of being forgotten. Forgotten by the one who gave them birth. Forgotten by the biological father whose name they may not even know. But most of all, forgotten by God.

Through searching the scriptures, I learned that far from being forgotten, the orphan is the object of God's special care and protection.

- He does what is necessary to preserve the orphan's life (Jeremiah 49: 11).
- He gladdens the orphan's heart with the bounty of providence (Deuteronomy 24:19).
- He feeds them from the 'sacred portion' (Deuteronomy 24: 19-21).
- He defends the cause of the fatherless, giving food and clothing (Deuteronomy 10: 18; Isaiah 1:17).
- He hears even the faintest of cries from the orphan. (Exodus 22:22-24)
- He becomes a father to them (Psalm 68:5).
- He considers helping orphans an unblemished act of worship (James 1:27).
- He provides what the orphan is searching for—love, pity and mercy (Hosea 14: 3).
- He blesses those who provide for the orphan (Deuteronomy 14:29).
- He has a unique plan for the orphan in history (Esther 2: 15).
- He strongly warns judges who issue unrighteous decrees and the magistrates who cause oppressive decisions against the orphan (Isaiah 10: 2; Malachi 3: 5).
- He is pleased when nations and people treat the orphan justly (Jeremiah 5: 28).
- He will draw nigh and be a swift witness against oppressors of the fatherless (Isaiah 10:2).
- He commands others not to remove the ancient boundary stone or encroach on the fields of the fatherless (Proverbs 23:10).

Which of the bulleted statements is most significant to you? Why?

_____

_____

Putting My Feelings and Needs into Words

1. When and where do you look for "the missing face?"

   _____

   _____

2. How do you feel when God says he is holding you *right now* in his everlasting arms and has been even before you were born?

   _____

   _____

3. Have you felt forgotten by God or others, such as your birth family, in the past? Explain.

   _____

   _____

4. What do you need the most from God right now?

   _____

   _____

Writing Letters TO and FROM My Birth Mother and My Adoptive Parents

- Write a letter TO your birth mother. Imagine that she is on her death bed and you are writing her one last time. What would you say?

- Write one last letter FROM your birth mother. How would she respond to your parting thoughts and what would she want you to know?

- Write a letter TO your adoptive parents, expressing your feelings toward them after working through this book.

- What do you think they would say to you, after learning what you have often What do you think they would say to you, after learning what you have often silently struggled with? Write a letter FROM them.

Letters TO and FROM
My Birth Mother

_____

_____

_____

_____

_____

_____

_____

_____

_____

_____

_____

_____

_____

_____

_____

_____

_____

_____

_____

Digging Deep for Answers to My Adoption Questions

1. Your birth mother gave you the gift of birth, but who gave you the gift of life? See I John 5: 11-12.

   _____

   _____

2. What is the secret of coming to terms with unanswered adoption questions? See Philippians 4: 11-12.

   _____

   _____

3. Where are the answers of all your adoption questions? See Deuteronomy 29: 29

   _____

   _____

4. How has your life changed as a result of this study?

   _____

   _____

Thoughts, Insights, Goals and Prayers

_____

_____

Several years ago, I (Beth) participated in a Bible study which asked us to complete a timeline of our life in 10 year segments, asking God to reveal to us all the spiritual mile markers in our lives…broken places, hurts, disappointments, accomplishments, and joyful times…to help us see that God had been there all along…His grace is sufficient. To accomplish this task, I discovered a very helpful tool for a "Timeline Template" pictured above through Microsoft. It's free, and it's very easy to use, the text boxes expand to whatever size you need, and the arrows on the boxes can be moved to any location on the timeline.

I have copied for you the link for this "Timeline Template." It really helped me to get my thoughts on paper, and God has used it to heal me in so many ways. Here's the link…

http://office.microsoft.com/en-us/templates/timeline-TC001016265.aspx

The Hebrew concept of time is like a person rowing a boat. We see where we have been, we back into the future. I can clearly see that God has been there with me all along. I am not stuck in the past, I am rowing into the future, moving forward, proactive, with my focus, my mindset, on God, who is sovereign. He sees the past, the present, and the future all-at-once. Morning after morning in my quiet time, I bring myself back to the Cross of Christ…as I bow before Him, I experience anew His forgiveness, redemption, mercy, and grace, as I sense His blood dripping over the Crown of Thorns pressed into His brow, onto my heart, covering my sin, and I get up from my knees wearing His Robe of righteousness as I face the day ahead…rowing into the future.

At last we have learned to see our adoption experience through God's eyes. How refreshing! You and I have been like the baby eaglet that learns to fly by flying first on the mighty wings of the mother eagle. Looking down upon your adoption experience as you fly, you can see that you truly were adopted for a purpose—his purpose!

Parting Thoughts
Fill your name in the blanks:
"For the Lord's portion is _____, _____ his allotted inheritance. In a desert he found _____, in a barren and howling waste. He shielded _____ and cared for _____ and guarded _____ as the apple of his eye, like an eagle that stirs up its nest and hovers over its young, that spreads its wings to catch them and carries them on its pinions" (Deuteronomy 32:11).

God bless you, dear friend for walking through this journey with me.

May you soar on!

A

Accepted
Afraid
Ambivalent
Angry
Anxious
Anxious to please others
Apathetic
Appreciated
Ashamed
Attractive
Awkward

B

Beaten
Beautiful
Betrayed
Bewildered
Bored
Brave

C

Calm
Cared for
Cautious
Cheated
Closed
Comfortable
Compassionate
Competent
Concerned
Confident
Confused
Connected
Contented
Cowardly
Cruel
Curious
Cut off

D

Defeated

Defensive
Depressed
Deprived
Deserving punishment
Desperate
Determined
Disappointed in self
Disappointed in others
Disconnected
Dishonored
Disrespected
Distant
Distracted
Distressed
Distrustful
Dominated

E

Eager
Embarrassed
Encouraged
Energetic
Envious
Ecstatic

F

Failure, like a
Fearful
Friendly
Friendless
Frustrated

G

Grateful
Grudge-bearing
Guilty
Gutless

H

Happy
Hateful

Honored
Hopeful
Hopeless
Hostile
Humorous
Hurt

I

Ignored
Immobilized
Impatient
Important
Inadequate
Incompetent
In control
Indecisive
Indifferent
Inferior
Inhibited
Insecure
Insignificant
Insincere
Intelligent
Invisible
Isolated

J

Jealous
Joyful
Judgmental

K

Kept
Kept at bay
Kept away
Kept in
kept out
kicked
kicked around
kind
kindhearted
knowledgeable

L
Lonely
Loser, like a
Loved
Loving
Loyal

M
Manipulated
Manipulative
Melancholy
Minimized
Misunderstood

N
Nasty
Needy
Neglected

O
Old beyond years
Optimistic
Out of control
Over-controlled
Overlooked
Overwhelmed

P
Paranoid
Peaceful
Persecuted
Pessimistic
Phony
Pleased
Pleased with self
Possessive
Pouty
Pressured
Proud

Q
Qualified
Quandary
Quarrelsome
Quiet

R
Real
Rejected
Repulsive
Respected
Restrained

S
Sad
Safe
Secure
Serene
Shocked
Shy
Sick
Silly
Sincere
Sinful
Sluggish
Soft
Sorry
Spirit-filled
Stressed
Stubborn
Stupid
Sunshiny
Superior
Supported
Suspicious
Sympathetic

T
Talented
Teased
Tenacious
Tender
Terrible
Terrific
Terrified
Thankful
Threatened
Torn
Touchy
Troubled
Trusting
Trustworthy

U
Ugly
Unable to communicate
Unaccepted
Unappreciated
Uncertain
Understanding
Understood
Unloved
Uptight
Used
Useless

V
Valuable
Victimized
Vindictive
Violent

W
Weary
Weepy
Winner, like a
Wishy-washy
Withdrawn
Wonderful
Worn down
Worthy
Wronged

X
Excellent
Excited

Y
Yearning
Yellow
Yielding
Young
Youthful

Z
Zany
Zealous

A

Advocate - 1 John 2:1
Alive for Evermore - Revelation 1:18
All-Knowing - Psalm 139:1-6
All, and in All - Colossians 3:11
Almighty - Revelation 1:8
Alpha and Omega - Revelation 1:8
Altar - Hebrews 13:10
Altogether Lovely - Song of Solomon 5:16
Amen - Revelation 3:14
Ancient of Days - Daniel 7:13 & Daniel 7:22
Anointed One - 1 Samuel 2:35
Author of Eternal Salvation - Hebrews 5:9
Author of our Faith - Hebrews 12:2

B

Balm of Gilead - Jeremiah 8:22
Banner over us - Ps 60:4 S of Sol 2:4
Bearer of Sin - Hebrews 9:28
Before All Things - Colossians 1:17
Beginning and Ending - Revelation 1:8
Bishop of our Souls - 1 Peter 2:25
Blessed and Only Potentate - 1 Timothy 6:15
Blessed Hope - Titus 2:13
Bread of Life, my manna - John 6:35
Bridegroom - John 3:29
Bright and Morning Star - Revelation 22:16
Brightness of His Glory - Hebrews 1:3
Buckler - Psalms 18:30

C

Captain - Joshua 5:14-15 - Hebrews 2:10
Changeless One - Malachi 3:6, Hebrews 13:8
Chief Among 10,000 - S. of Solomon 5:10
Chosen of God - 1 Peter 2:4
Christ - Matthew 1:16 - 1 John 5:1
Comforter - John 14:16-18
Consolation of Israel - Luke 2:25
Counselor - Isaiah 9:6
Creator - Romans 1:25 - Isaiah 40:28
Crown of Glory - Isaiah 28:5

D

Daystar to Arise - 2 Peter 1:19
Defense - Psalms 94:22
Deliverer - Psalms 40:17
Desire of all Nations - Haggai 2:7
Despised and rejected - Ps 22:6, Is 53:3
Diadem of Beauty - Isaiah 28:5
Door of the Sheep - John 10:7
Dwelling Place - Psalms 90:1

E

Emmanuel - Matthew 1:23
End of the Law - Romans 10:4
Ensign of the People - Isaiah 11:10
Equal with God - Philippians 2:6
Eternal God - Deuteronomy 33:27
Eternal Life - 1 John 1:2
Everlasting Father - Isaiah 9:6

F

Faithful and True - Rev 19:11 - Rev 3:14
Finisher of the Faith - Hebrews 12:2
First Begotten - Hebrews 1:6 - Romans 8:29
Firstfruit of Them Sleep - 1 Cor 15:20 Rom 11:16
Fortress - Psalms 18:2
Foundation Which is Laid - 1 Cor. 3:11
Fountain of Living Waters - Jer 17:13 Ps 36:9
Friend of Publicans and Sinners - Luke 7:34
Friend Sticks Closer than a Brother - Prov. 18:24

G

Gift of God - John 4:10
Glory, my and lifter of my head - Psalms 3:3
God Who Avenges Me - Psalms 18:47
God Blessed Forever - Romans 9:5
God Who Forgives - Psalms 99:8
God of My Life - Psalms 42:8
God in the Midst of Her - Psalms 46:5
God manifest in the flesh - 1 Timothy 3:16
God of My Righteousness - Psalms 4:1
God of My Salvation - Psalms 18:46
God of My Strength - Psalms 43:2
God With Us - Matthew 1:23
Good Shepherd - John 10:11
Gracious - Ex 33:19, Rom 16:24, Rev. 22:21
Great God - Titus 2:13
Great Shepherd of the Sheep - Hebrews 13:20
Guide Even Unto Death - Psalms 48:14

H

Harmless - Hebrews 7:26
Head of all Principality & Power - Col 2:10
Heir of All Things - Hebrews 1:2
Helper - Hebrews 13:6
Hiding Place - Psalms 32:7
High Priest Forever - Hebrews 6:20
High Tower - Psalms 18:2
Holy One Of Israel - Psalms 89:18
Horn of Salvation - Luke 1:69
Husband - Revelation 21:2

I

I Am - John 18:6
Image of the Invisible God - Colossians 1:15
Immanuel - Isaiah 7:14
Inhabiter of Eternity - Isaiah 57:15
Inhabiter of Praises - Psalms 22:3
Intercessor - Isaiah 53:12 & Romans 8:34

J

Jehovah Jireh - Provider - I Jn 4:9, Philip 4:19
Jehovah Nissi - Banner - I Chronicles 29:11-13
Jehovah Shalom - Peace - Is 9:6, Rom 8:31-35
Jehovah Tsidkenu - Righteousness - I Cor 1:30
Jehovah Shammah - Present - Hebrews 13:5
Jehovah M'Kaddesh - Sanctifier - I Cor 1:30
Jehovah Rophe - Healer - Isaiah 53:4,5
Jehovah Rohi - Shepherd - Psalm 23
Jesus - Matthew 1:21
Jesus Christ Our Lord - Romans 7:25
Judge of All - Genesis 18:25 - Acts 10:42
Just One - Acts 7:52

K

Keeper - Psalms 121:5
King Eternal - 1 Timothy 1:17
King Immortal - 1 Timothy 1:17
King Invisible - 1 Timothy 1:17
King of Glory - Psalms 24:7-8
King of Heaven - Daniel 4:37
King of Kings - Revelation 19:16
King of Peace - Hebrews 7:2
King of Righteousness - Hebrews 7:2
King of Saints - Revelation 15:3

L

Lamb of God - John 1:29 - Rev 17:14
Lamb Slain - Rev 13:8 - Rev 5:12 - Rev 7:17
Last Adam - 1 Cor.15:45
Lawgiver - James 4:12
Life - John 14:6
Lifter of Mine Head - Psalms 3:3
Light - John 1:7
Light of the World - John 8:12
Lily of the Valleys - Song of Solomon 2:1
Lion of the Tribe of Judah - Revelation 5:5
Living Bread - John 6:51
Lord and My God - John 20:28
Lord and Savior - 2 Peter 1:11
Lord of the Dead and the Living - Rom 14:9
Lord God Almighty - Revelation 16:7
Lord God Omnipotent - Revelation 19:6
Lord Jesus Christ - James 2:1
Lord of Glory - 1 Cor.2:8
Lord of the Harvest - Matthew 9:38
Lord of Lords - 1 Timothy 6:15

M

Maker - Psalms 95:6
Man of Sorrows - Isaiah 53:3
Master - Matthew 23:10
Mediator - 1 Timothy 2:5
Merciful - Heb 2:17
Messiah the Prince - Daniel 9:25
Mighty God - Isaiah 9:6
Morning Star - Revelation 2:28

N

Name Above Every Name - Philippians 2:9
Nazarene - Matthew 2:23

O

Omega - Revelation 22:13
Omnipotent - Revelation 19:6
Only Begotten Son - John 3:16
Only Potentate - 1 Timothy 6:15
Only Wise God - 1 Timothy 1:17

P

Passover, my - 1 Cor.5:7
Pavilion - Psalms 31:20
Peace, our - Ephesians 2:14
Physician, great - Luke 4:23
Portion of Mine Inheritance - Psalms 16:5
Potter - Jeremiah 18:6
Power of God - 1 Cor.1:24
Preeminent one - Colossians 1:18

Q

Quick Understanding - Isaiah 11:3
Quickening Spirit - 1 Cor.15:45

R

Rabbi - John 3:2
Ransom for Many - Matthew 20:28
Redeemer - Job 19:25 - 1 Cor.1:30
Refiner - Malachi 3:2
Refuge in Trouble - Ps 46:1, Ps 9:9
Refuge from the Storm - Is 25:4
Resting Place - Jeremiah 50:6
Resurrection and the Life - John 11:25
Reward of the Righteous - Psalms 58:11
Righteous Judge - 2 Timothy 4:8
Righteousness, my - 1 Cor.1:30 - Rom 10:3
Rock that is Higher than I - Psalms 61:2
Rock of My Refuge - Psalms 94:22
Rock of Our Salvation - Psalms 95:1
Root and Offspring of David - Revelation 22:16
Rose of Sharon - Song of Solomon 2:1

S

Sacrifice for Sins - Hebrews 10:12
Salvation, my - Psalms 27:1
Same Yesterday, Today, Forever - Heb 13:8
Savior of the Body - Ephesians 5:23
Savior of the World - John 4:42
Scapegoat - Leviticus 16:8 & John 11:49-52
Scepter of Israel - Numbers 24:17
Sent One - John 9:4
Separate from Sinners - Hebrews 7:26
Serpent in the Wilderness - John 3:14
Shadow of the Almighty - Psalms 91:1
Shadow of a Great Rock - Isaiah 32:2
Shelter - Psalms 61:3
Shepherd, my - Psalms 23:1
Shield - Psalms 84:9
Sin, for us - 2 Cor.5:21
Son of God - John 1:49
Son of Man - John 1:51
Song, my - Isaiah 12:2
Spiritual Rock - 1 Cor.10:4
Star out of Jacob - Numbers 24:17
Stone the Builders Rejected - Matthew 21:42
Strength of My Life - Psalms 27:1
Stronghold in the Day of Trouble - Nahum 1:7

Strong Tower - Proverbs 18:10
Stronger than the enemy - Luke 11:22
Sun of Righteousness - Malachi 4:2

T

Tabernacle of God - Revelation 21:3
Tender Plant - Isaiah 53:2
Testator - Hebrews 9:16
Treasure - 2 Cor.4:7
True Bread from Heaven - John 6:32
True Light - John 1:9
True Vine - John 15:1 Truth - John 14:6

U

Undefiled - Hebrews 7:26
Unspeakable Gift - 2 Cor.9:15
Upholder of All things - Hebrews 1:3
Upright - Psalms 92:15

V

Very God of Peace - 1 Thessalonians 5:23
Very Present Help in Trouble - Psalms 46:1
Victory - 1 Cor.15:54 Vine - John 15:5
Voice - Revelation 1:12

W

Way - John 14:6
Well of Living Waters - John 4:14
Wisdom of God - 1 Cor.1:24
Wise Master Builder - 1 Cor.3:10
Witness of God - 1 John 5:9
Wonderful - Isaiah 9:6
Word - John 1:1 - Revelation 19:13
Worthy - Revelation 4:11
Worthy Name - James 2:7

X

Exceeding Great Reward - Genesis 15:1
Excellency - Job 13:11
Excellency of Our God - Isaiah 35:2
Excellent - Psalms 8:1
Express Image of His Person - Hebrews 1:3

Y

Yes and Amen - 2 Cor 1:20
Young Child - Matthew 2:11

Z

Zeal of the Lord of Hosts - Isaiah 37:32
Zeal of your House - John 2:17

Suggested Support Group Format

Time Allotment: 1 ½ Hours

OPENING:

"Hi! My name is _____, and I am the facilitator for this group. I am so glad you came! I know it's often tough for us as adoptees to enter new groups. Your hands might be sweating and your mouth may be dry, but let me assure you that you are not alone."

INTRODUCTIONS:

"Let's begin by introducing ourselves to the group. I'll get the ball rolling. As I said, my name is _____ and I was adopted at _____ of age and grew up in _____. I am a _____ by profession."

(For subsequent weeks, the leader should ask if there are any new members. If so, have them introduce themselves and then do group introductions.)

EXPLAIN GUIDELINES:

"We have a few group guidelines that will keep us on the right track. If you get off track, I will gently remind you by saying something like, 'I think we're getting stuck here.'

The guidelines are:

1. Don't feel any pressure to share--it's perfectly acceptable to just listen.
2. No advice should be given unless requested.
3. All experiences will be honored.
4. What is shared must remain confidential.
5. We will begin and end on time."

LET'S BEGIN:

"Now, let's open our workbooks to page ____. The title of this chapter is _____. I will read each section heading and question and then ask you to respond whenever the time seems appropriate. We're not in a rush, so just relax as we begin."

DISCUSSION:

Move the group through each chapter section by asking questions like, "Who would like to share from this section?" Or, "Who had a good time on this question and would like to share?" If discussion takes a different direction than you expected, don't stress! You want your group to be spontaneous!

CLOSING:

"What a great time we've had! Thanks so much for what you shared with the group tonight. We will close our meeting by saying the Lord's Prayer together. Let's bow our heads…Our Father, who art in heaven, hallowed be thy name. Thy kingdom come, thy will be done on earth as it is in heaven. Give us this day our daily bread, and forgive us our trespasses as we forgive those who trespassed against us. Lead us not into temptation, but deliver us from evil. For thine is the kingdom, and the power, and the glory forever. Amen!"

DISMISS: "Have a great week! I encourage you to connect with other group members. You can make arrangements now by exchanging phone numbers, e-mail addresses or planning a lunch together. I will see you next week. Same time. Same place."

12 Daily Healing Steps For Adopted, Foster, & Orphan Children's Hearts

1. **We acknowledge we are powerless over the painful feeling inside that something is not right, and are willing to consider adoption loss a contributing factor. (I admit that I am often overwhelmed by the feeling that 'something inside just doesn't feel right')** "I know that nothing good lives in me, that is, in my sinful nature. For I have the desire to do what is good, but I cannot carry it out." Romans 7:18

2. **We realize that only a power greater than ourselves can enable us to rise above this inner chaos. (I realize that only someone stronger than me can help the mixed-up feelings go away)** "For it is God who works in you to will and to act according to his good purpose." Philippians 2:13

3. **We turn our wills and lives over the care of God as we understand Him, asking Him to give us the ability to trust Him and others. (I ask God to take care of me and help me learn to trust Him)** "Therefore, I urge you, brothers, in view of God's mercy, to offer your bodies as living sacrifices, holy and pleasing to God – this is your spiritual act of worship." Romans 12:1

4. **We make a searching and fearless moral inventory of ourselves. (I look deep in my heart and discover how I have hurt God, others, and myself)** "Let us examine our ways and test them, and let us return to the Lord." Lamentations 3:40

5. **We admit to God, ourselves, and another human being, the exact nature of our shortcomings. (I tell God and a person that I trust exactly how I have hurt others.)** "Therefore confess your sins to each other and pray for each other so that you may be healed." James 5:16

6. **We investigate the claim that Jesus Christ provided payment for our shortcomings. (I ask God to take away how bad I feel about hurting Him and others.)** "Humble yourselves before the Lord, and he will lift you up." James 4:10

7. **We humbly ask God how to receive the true Spirit of adoption. (I ask God how I can become His child.)** "If we confess our sins, he is faithful and just and will forgive us our sins and purify us from all unrighteousness." 1 John 1:9

8. **We make a list of all persons we have harmed, and are willing to make amends to them all. (I make a list of everyone I have hurt and need to apologize to.).** "Do to others as you would have them do to you." Luke 6:31

9. **We make direct amends to such people whenever possible, except when to do so would injure them or others. (I go to the people I have hurt and say I am sorry, unless it would hurt them or someone else.)** "Therefore, if you are offering your gift at the altar and there remember that your brother has something against you, leave your gift there in front of the altar. First go and be reconciled to your brother; then come and offer your gift." Matthew 5:23-24

10. **We continue to take personal inventory, and when wrong, promptly admit it. (I keep track every day of how I hurt others and ask them right away to forgive me.)** "So, if you think you are standing firm, be careful that you don't fall." 1 Corinthians 10:12

11. **We daily seek to deepen our intimacy with God through prayer and meditation on truth, and discover God's plan for our lives. (I try every day to get to know God by reading the Bible, praying, and being with other Christians.)** "Let the word of Christ dwell in you richly."Col. 3:16

12. **We seek to carry the message of grace and hope to those who are still hurting. (I reach out to those that are still hurting and live daily as Jesus would.)** "Brothers, if someone is caught in a sin, you who are spiritual should restore him gently. But watch yourself, or you also may be tempted." Galatians 6:1

Made in the USA
San Bernardino, CA
22 May 2020

72127068R00080